PARKINSON'S & RECREATION 2

NO WALK IN THE PARKINSON'S

DENNIS JERNIGAN

SHEPHERD'S HEART MUSIC, INC.

DENNIS JERNIGAN

Published by Dennis Jernigan/Shepherd's Heart Music

7804 Fern Mountain Road

Muskogee, OK 74401

No part of this publication may be reproduced in any form without the written permission of the publisher except in the case of brief quotations within critical articles and reviews.

©2025 Dennis Jernigan

Jernigan, Dennis: Parkinson's & Recreation 2 — No Walk In The Parkinson's

ISBN (paperback): 978-1-948772-23-5

ISBN (epub): 978-1-948772-24-2

ISBN (hardcover): 978-1-948772-25-9

Cover Design; Jones House Creative

Edited by: Darren Thornberry

Interior Design: Bo Elder

All songs (words and music) written by Dennis Jernigan unless otherwise noted.

To my wife…for fighting for me and with me; to my children and their spouses…for helping me be a better dad; to my grandchildren…for bringing the hope love, and life found in knowing Jesus to a new generation; to All In All Church…for having my back; to all who experience life with Parkinson's or any type of affliction…for being the bearers of hope; to my Savior and Lord, Jesus Christ…for giving me grace to endure…

PROLOGUE
SHAKE, RATTLE, AND ROLL

As I begin this journey of putting pen to paper, I can't help but reflect on the common phrase we've all heard—"a walk in the park." The mere mention of those words conjures up images of a leisurely stroll through a lush, verdant oasis, the gentle breeze rustling the leaves overhead and the melodic chirping of birds providing a soothing soundtrack. Ah, the assumption that such an activity is pleasant and stress-free.

Well, let me tell you, my friends—Parkinson's disease is about as far from a "walk in the park" as you can get. In fact, it's more akin to navigating a minefield while juggling chainsaws, all while someone is poking you with a sharp stick. Okay, maybe that's a bit of an exaggeration, but you get the idea. Parkinson's is neither easy nor stress-free, that's for sure.

But you know what I believe? Parkinson's can be an excuse to do wild, outrageous things and get away with it! And let me tell you, I've taken that to heart. Trembling hands? No problem—I'll just blame it on the Parkinson's when I accidentally spill my morning coffee all over my crisp, white shirt. Struggling to keep up with the grandkids? "Sorry, kids, Grandpa's got the Parkinson's shuffle going on today. Race you to the couch!"

While Parkinson's may not be the leisurely "walk in the park" that the idiom suggests, I've learned to approach it with a joyful attitude. I embrace the challenges, find the humor in the chaos, and make the most of this wild and unpredictable journey.

In the grand dance of life, I never imagined I'd be leading with the Parkinson's Two-Step. But as fate would have it, I found myself thrust onto a stage where the choreography is unpredictable, the music a mix of triumph and challenge, and the audience a blend of sympathy and admiration.

Let me set the scene: a seemingly ordinary day, much like any other. The sun was shining, the birds were chirping, and I was...well, I was shaking like a leaf in a windstorm. No, I wasn't nervous (at least not yet). I was just getting acquainted with my new dance partner— Parkinson's disease.

It wasn't the partner I had envisioned for myself. I had always pictured a graceful waltz through life, gliding effortlessly from one moment to the next. But Parkinson's had other ideas. It has a penchant for throwing in unexpected twists and turns, leaving me stumbling and bumbling my way through each day.

Now, don't get me wrong. I'm not one to wallow in self-pity or lament the hand I've been dealt. If anything, I've learned to embrace the absurdity of it all. I mean, who wouldn't find humor in trying to butter toast with hands that have a mind of their own? Or attempting to pour a cup of coffee without turning it into a Jackson Pollock masterpiece?

But amidst the laughter and the lighthearted moments, there are also days when Parkinson's has me feeling like I am stuck in a never-ending game of Whac-A-Mole. Just when I think I have one symptom under control, another pops up to take its place. It's enough to make even the most stoic among us want to throw in the towel.

But here's the thing about Parkinson's: It may have thrown me a curveball, but it has also taught me a thing or two about resilience. It showed me that even when life hands you a shaky hand, you can still find joy in the little victories, like managing to tie your shoes without tying yourself in knots or making it through a meal without wearing more of it than you eat.

So, consider this book a backstage pass to the greatest show on earth—the rollercoaster ride that is life with Parkinson's. We'll laugh, we'll cry, and we'll probably spill a few cups of coffee along the way. But hey, isn't that what makes life worth living?

So, grab a seat, buckle up, and get ready to shake, rattle, and roll your way through the pages ahead. Trust me, it's going to be one heck of a ride.

ONE
PROGRESS VS. PROGRESSION

"Progress is impossible without change, and those who cannot change their minds cannot change anything."

— GEORGE BERNARD SHAW

"I don't harp on the negative because if you do, then there's no progression. There's no forward movement. You got to always look on the bright side of things, and we are in control. Like, you have control over the choices you make."

— TARAJI P. HENSON

You know, it's funny how the very words we use to describe our journey through life—progress, progression—can take on such a different meaning when you're staring down the barrel of a Parkinson's diagnosis. As I write this, my right hand trembling ever so slightly, I can't help but chuckle at the irony of it all.

Progress, they say, is all about moving forward, onward, toward some grand destination. But for me, it's become more about simply putting one foot in front of the other, day by day, as I navigate this new and ever-changing landscape. And progression? Well, that's a whole other beast, isn't it? A gradual, relentless march toward a more "advanced" state of being, which, in my case, translates to a slow, almost imperceptible unraveling of the very things that once made me, well, me.

But you know, I've learned to find the humor in it all. Like the other day, when I spilled my morning coffee all over my lap because my hands decided to have a mind of their own. Or that time I got the giggles during a particularly solemn church service, much to the bewilderment of my fellow parishioners. It's all part of the dance, I suppose—this delicate balance between the sacred and the profane, the tragic and the comedic.

And through it all, my eyes remain fixed on that ultimate destination —life with Jesus. It's the light at the end of the tunnel, the promise of something greater, something more eternal than this mortal coil. And as I stumble and fumble my way toward that final rendezvous, I can't help but feel a sense of...well, not exactly peace, but something akin to it. A deep, abiding acceptance of the journey, no matter how bumpy or unpredictable it may be.

So, here I am, six years into this wild ride, and I've developed a pretty keen sense of what this progression of Parkinson's looks like. It's like watching a slow-motion train wreck, really—a gradual unraveling of the self, a steady erosion of the things that once made me whole.

PARKINSON'S & RECREATION 2

But through it all, I'm learning to find the joy, the laughter, and the grace in the most unexpected of places.

Alright, let's be real here: Parkinson's is making its presence known in this ol' bod of mine. But you know what? I've made some pretty darn good progress in how I'm dealing with all of this. It's like I've got this secret weapon in my arsenal, and his name is Jesus.

You see, I've come to this realization that God doesn't waste a single thing—not my wounds, not my sorrows, not even my epic failures. Nope, he takes it all and turns it into something beautiful. He's like a master sculptor, and I'm the clay. He's chipping away, shaping me, molding me into the person he wants me to be. And let me tell you, the final product is going to be a real showstopper.

Now, I know what you're thinking: *If God is so good and loving, why on earth would he let Parkinson's invade your life?* Well, my friend, that's the million-dollar question, isn't it? But I'm not God. I'm just little ol' me, trying my best to navigate this crazy world. And you know what? I'm cool with that. Because I know that his ways are higher than mine, and his thoughts are way more awesome than anything I could ever come up with.

So, when the tremors kick in, or I can't quite remember why I entered a room, I take a deep breath and remind myself that I'm not alone. Jesus is right there with me, holding my hand, whispering, "Hey, I got this. Just trust me, will ya?"

And I do. I trust Him with every fiber of my being. Because I know that He wants nothing but the best for me. Even when I was just a sinner, stumbling through life, He loved me. And when He invited me to be born again, well, that's when the real fun began. Suddenly, I was learning to think like Him, to see the world through His eyes. And the view is pretty darn spectacular.

So, yeah, Parkinson's is making its way through my body, but I'm not going down without a fight. I'm going to keep on laughing, keep on trusting, and keep on letting Jesus work his wonders. Because at the end of the day, I know that He's got this. And that, my friends, is the best progress I could ever hope for.

You know, one of the things I love most about our good Lord is that He's got this incredible ability to see the big picture, while also homing in on the tiniest of details. It's like He's got these cosmic-sized binoculars, but He can also zoom in and spot the most minuscule speck on the horizon.

And when it comes to this ol' noggin of mine, He's definitely not missing a thing. I mean, the day I was born again, it was like someone hit the reset button on my brain. Suddenly, all those old thought patterns and ways of seeing myself—the negative, the self-deprecating, the downright ridiculous—were staring me right in the face, begging to be dealt with.

But I didn't just let them slide. No, I went straight to the source, cracked open the Bible, and started soaking up the truth of who God says I am. And it's been a wild ride ever since.

One minute, I'm sitting there, mentally beating myself up over some silly mistake, and the next, I'm hearing this booming voice in my head: "Dennis Jernigan, you listen here! You are a child of the Most High God, created in My image, loved beyond measure!"

PARKINSON'S & RECREATION 2

When the Almighty starts throwing around my full name like that, you better believe I sit up and pay attention.

But Dennis, you're 66 years old! you might be thinking. *Surely, by now, you've got this whole "renewing the mind" thing down to a science.* Well, it's a process, my friends. Just when I think I've got it all figured out, God throws me a curveball, using something as simple as a trembling hand or a momentary lapse in memory to remind me that I'm still very much a work in progress.

But I wouldn't have it any other way because I know that everything He allows in my life—every challenge, every triumph, every moment of sheer absurdity—is all part of His grand plan to help me see myself the way He sees me.

So, if you ever catch me muttering under my breath, "Dennis Jernigan, you magnificent, God-created, love-drenched child of the King, you better start acting like it!" just know that I'm doing my best to stay on track, to keep my eyes fixed on the truth of who I am in Christ. Because that's the only thing that really matters. Well, that and a good sense of humor to get me through the inevitable spilled coffee and lost car keys.

Let's take a trip down memory lane, shall we? I'm talking way back to when I was just a newborn babe, a diamond in the rough, if you will. You see, this whole diamond-making process ain't for the faint of heart. It's like the Master Jeweler up there has got his tools out, and He's going to town, sanding and chipping and hammering away at every one of my rough edges. And sometimes it feels like He's being a little heavy-handed, you know? Like, "Slow down there, Big Guy! I'm delicate, remember?"

But then I remember this is the same God who knit me together in my mother's womb. He knows exactly what He's doing. He's the one who's going to turn this rough-and-tumble, shaky-handed, perpetually-lost-car-keys version of me into a priceless, one-of-a-kind masterpiece. And I'm more than okay with that.

Enter Parkinson's, stage left. Now, I'll be the first to admit this particular tool of the Master Jeweler has made me feel, well, a little rough around the edges. I mean, the tremors, the forgetfulness, the constant "Where did I put my coffee?" moments are enough to make a fella want to throw in the towel.

But I've got this solid rock, this firm foundation, this True North to keep me grounded. And His name is Jesus. Because if there's one thing I know for certain, it's that this God of mine loves me. He loves me more than I could ever fathom. And He's not going to let a little thing like Parkinson's derail his plans for me.

So, when the going gets tough, when I feel like I'm being hammered and chipped and sanded down to the core, I remember this is how the Master Jeweler is going to turn this rough diamond into something truly spectacular. And you better believe I'm going to be shining brighter than a freshly polished Rolex when He's done with me.

As I sit here and reflect on this journey I've been on, I can't help but be absolutely floored by the sheer beauty and complexity of it all.

PARKINSON'S & RECREATION 2

And the facets—oh, the facets! I've got joy that just bubbles up in dire circumstances, like a little giggle-inducing spring in the middle of a desert. I've got love and hope that can light up even the darkest of souls, like a beacon in the night. And don't even get me started on the facets of laughter, humility, and forgiveness. Those bad boys just defy all human logic, yet here they are, sparkling away for all to see.

Now, I used to be able to tickle the ivories like nobody's business, and now I'm lucky if I can find the darn keys to my car. But you know what? I'm not letting that define me. Nope, I'm taking a page out of the Master Jeweler's book and using it as another opportunity to be refined, to be shaped into something even more spectacular.

Because this isn't about me and my measly piano-playing skills. It's about shining the light of Christ in a way that no one else can. It's about being a beacon of hope and joy and laughter in a world that's all too often bogged down by the harsh realities of life. And I'm going to keep on sparkling, no matter how many times I retrace my steps to find that darn cup of coffee.

So, here I am, trying to lead worship for our little home group, and my fingers are starting to mutiny on me. I mean, who needs three whole fingers anyway, right? Nah, I'm just going to get creative and use these trusty old thumbs and forefingers to get the job done. And it's working! The voices are still soaring, the melodies are still ringing out, and no one is the wiser that I'm a two-finger wonder up here.

But let's not forget about the other battle scar I've picked up along the way—my voice. Oh, my voice. It used to be this smooth, velvety tenor that could make the angels weep (at least in my mind!). Now? It's more like a cross between a bullfrog and a broken kazoo. But I'm not going to let that stop me. I'm just going to transpose everything down a few keys and let my raspy whisper-voice do the singing. Because at the end of the day, it's not about me and my vocal prowess. It's about lifting up the name of Jesus, and I'm going to do that until my last breath, even if it sounds like I'm gargling gravel.

And can we talk about the fact that I've recorded more than 40 albums over the years? Talk about a life well-lived! From high school choir to the Christian trio to leading worship, I've been singing my heart out for over 46 years. And now, Parkinson's comes in and tries to steal my thunder. But I'm going to keep on singing, even if I have to do it in a higher key or with the grace and elegance of a drunken sailor.

And let's talk about these facial tremors, shall we? Talk about a real confidence-killer. I mean, I'll be trying to strike up a conversation with someone new, and suddenly it's like my face is auditioning for a part in a Michael J. Fox movie. But you know what? I've learned that people are pretty darn understanding when they find out I've got Parkinson's. It's almost like they see right through the tremors and into the heart of this old, slightly wobbly guy who's just trying his best to live life to the fullest.

And speaking of living life to the fullest, let me tell you about my grandkids. Oh, those little rascals, they keep me on my toes. I may not be able to chase them around the backyard like I used to, but I'm still giving it my all. We're talking baseball, tag, frisbee, the whole nine yards. Sure, I may need to take a breather every now and then, and I might take a tumble or two while trying to catch a ball, but my grandkids are champs. They've learned to be patient with Grandpa and his Parkinson's, and they even teach me a thing or two about respecting my elders. It's like they're the ones leading the charge when it comes to progress, not me.

Parkinson's may be slowing me down, but I'm going to keep on singing, keep on playing, keep on chasing those grandkids around, because life is for living to the fullest, come what may.

And then there are those moments when one of my grandkids comes strolling into my room, gives me the biggest hug they can muster, and asks if there's anything I need. And you know what I always say? "Nothing except you."

My grandkids don't see this Parkinson's-riddled grandpa; they just see their beloved grandpa, and they make sure I know it. "You're the best grandpa in the world!" they'll say.

I always try to one up them: "I love you more!"

But they always win: "That's not possible! I love you bigger than the universe!"

Progress, my friends, pure progress.

The more this Parkinson's tries to take from me, the more I seem to gain in other areas. I may look like a bit of a diamond in the rough these days, but those facets of who and whose I am shine brighter than ever. It's all about perspective, you see. I could sit around and play the victim, but where's the fun in that? Nah, I'd much rather focus on taking care of this old body of mine, finding purpose and meaning in each new day, and fighting for the people I love.

So, if you ever find yourself feeling down and out, just remember this Parkinson's-fighting, grandkid-loving, music-making machine, and know that if I can do it, you can too. I'm going to keep on making progress, one day, one hug, one song at a time.

TWO
SEASONS

"All my boyhood, all I ever wanted was to be loved."

— NORMAN WISDOM

This beautiful quote perfectly encapsulates the essence of longing we all have for connection and love. It reminds me of a poignant scene from *Indiana Jones and the Dial of Destiny* where Indiana Jones and Dean Charles Stanforth reflect on the losses they've endured:

Indiana Jones: "Brutal couple of years, huh, Charlie? First Dad, then Marcus."

Dean Charles Stanforth: "We seem to have reached the age where life stops giving us things and starts taking them away."

After the unexpected success of my previous book, "Parkinson's & Recreation: One Man's Journey Through Parkinson's...So Far," I decided to embark on writing volume two. I find myself in a bit of a pickle. Am I driven to write because the first book helped so many, or is this a compulsive need to document every new, quirky symptom of Parkinson's disease?

The first book was the No. 1 new release on Amazon in April 2023 in the Parkinson's disease category and even climbed to No. 2 on the bestseller list. In my mind, that's quite the triumph!

When this second book hits the shelves, I'll be 66 years old, edging closer to what society calls the "golden years." Truth be told, these days, just waking up to see another day feels golden enough for me.

As I pondered the best way to start this book, a flood of humorous memories from my past came rushing in. Some of these stories are so outlandish that even I can't believe they happened, but hey, I'm an old guy now! I can say whatever I darn well please, and if people shake their heads and mutter, "Don't mind him, he's just an old guy," so be it.

Reflecting on my life, I see it divided into distinct seasons. My younger days were the spring of my life—full of budding potential. The ages of 20 to 45 were my summer—vibrant and productive. The autumn of my life spanned from 45 to 59, filled with rich experiences. Since my diagnosis with Parkinson's on January 28, 2019, I've entered the winter. My aim is to share humorous, nostalgic, and joyful memories to encourage you through your own seasons.

I toyed with subtitling this book "Seasons," but as I reminisced, I realized my life is a grand adventure—a magnificent saga where I plan to ride off into the sunset, living each day as if it were my last. Or better yet, living each day as a Bonus Day! Waking up each morning feels like winning the jackpot.

In his insightful book, "The Way of the Wild Heart," John Eldredge beautifully describes the six stages of a man's life. I won't pretend to match Eldredge's eloquence, but his words have helped me see that every experience, even the disappointments and suffering, have shaped me.

Stage One: *Boyhood*

This is when a young boy needs to know his father delights in him. To be honest, I didn't believe my dad loved me when I was a boy. He never told me "I love you" until long after I was married.

I remember asking him, "Why did you never tell me you loved me when I was growing up?"

His response? "My dad never told me he loved me, so I didn't know how to tell you." That simple answer transported me from feeling like a lost boy to understanding true manhood.

Stage Two: *The Cowboy*

Adolescence is a time of adventure and learning the value of hard work. I spent countless hours riding my trusty horse, Sugar, and milking cows twice a day. I recall spraying our herd for parasites, vaccinating them, and castrating baby calves. It was no ball for them…literally! I also remember jumping off 50-foot cliffs into a local shale pit and swinging from a rope swing high enough to do flips. My brothers and cousins and I raced our horses across fields with reckless abandon, our eyes watering from the speed.

This reckless spirit carried into my college days—like the time a buddy and I went skydiving just to say we did it, or the week we camped in the Sangre de Cristo Mountains of Southwestern Colorado. We explored a narrow crevice in a cave, climbed near the summit of a 12,000-foot peak, and got caught in a thunderstorm, diving for cover just as lightning struck nearby. Back then, I believed I could do anything. "Cowboy up," as they say, and if being a cowboy requires two balls, well, I suppose I qualified.

Stage Three: *The Warrior*

From around 19 to the early 20s, young men need a mission. My mission was simple: I wanted to be a songwriter. This may not sound grand, but for me, it was everything. Despite my university music department head telling me they didn't see potential in me, I pursued songwriting anyway. Less than 10 years later, my songs were sung in churches worldwide. It just goes to show, God sees potential where people often cannot.

Stage Four: *The Lover*

I never imagined I'd marry a woman, as I struggled with same-sex attraction (SSA) until I graduated college. But on November 7, 1981, at a Christian rock concert, I felt God's love so profoundly that it changed my self-perception. I made a simple proposition to God: "If You want me to be married, speak through my parents."

Shortly after, during a visit home, my parents expressed their belief that Melinda was the one for me. Despite chickening out and rephrasing the proposition to include Melinda's parents, their response was the same. Long story short, Melinda intercepted my letter to her mom, read it aloud, and after receiving her mom's blessing, we were engaged a month later and married a year after that. We now have nine children, and no, we're not Catholic, we're not Mormon, they're not adopted, and yes, we know what causes that! Even after 40 years, we still enjoy "that."

Stage Five: *The King*

From 40 to 60, a man's character and heart shape his power, financial gain, and influence. This stage of my life was a whirlwind as God sent my music and story around the world. I experienced the most beautiful and difficult moments of my life, which I call my grand adventure. The king stage ended when I was diagnosed with Parkinson's, just 13 days before my 60th birthday. One moment I was on the mountaintop and the next I was in the valley of despair. But God walked with me through the valley, revealing that as long as I had breath, there was one last stage for me.

Stage Six: *The Sage*

Starting in a man's early 60s and extending through his final days, this stage involves stepping aside and offering wisdom to younger generations. Despite Parkinson's trying to make me feel less wise, I look back and see the magnificence and beauty of my journey. Even with my flaws, God has turned my failures into blessings. Being a king allows you to see life from a throne, but being a sage lets you view life from the highest mountain peak, where real life happens in the valleys below.

We all experience different seasons, and I have cherished each one. From the springtime of birth through the summer of productivity, the autumn of richness to the winter days by the fireplace with my wife, I am grateful for every moment. Embrace each season, for joy lies in the journey.

Now, let's dive into some of those moments—those walks with Parkinson's—that have filled my life with laughter and love. Life can still be enjoyed as a "walk in the Parkinson's."

THREE
HOLDING ONTO YOUTH AND OTHER MYTHS

"The longer I've lived, the more I have realized living isn't measured in years. It's measured in moments. The ones we treasure all the more because they're fleeting. And in the end, all we are is the sum of choices we make in those moments. It's measured in meaning, in impact, and the people whose lives we touch."

— ALEC MERCER
(AS PLAYED BY ACTOR JESSE L MARTIN),
THE IRRATIONAL

"In youth we learn; in age we understand."

— MARIE VON EBNER-ESCHENBACH

"I live in that solitude which is painful in youth, but delicious in the years of maturity."

— ALBERT EINSTEIN

"The glory of young men is their strength, and the honor of old men is their gray hair."

— PROVERBS 20:29 NASB

"Your adornment must not be merely the external—braiding the hair, wearing gold jewelry, or putting on apparel; but it should be the hidden person of the heart, with the imperishable quality of a gentle and quiet spirit, which is precious in the sight of God."

—1 PETER 3:3-4 NASB

One of the most painful and embarrassing things about Parkinson's is the shame I sometimes feel when I realize my outward symptoms are attracting attention. I feel "less than." Less than a man. Less than able-bodied. Less than mentally keen.

It's not guilt. I know I haven't done something wrong. It's not shame. I don't believe that I AM something wrong. It's something far more sinister than either of these. It's pride—"the quality of having an excessively high opinion of oneself or one's importance."

When faced with pride, one must recognize that there is only one way to defeat the beast. Humble yourself. Pride would say, "You don't deserve to have PD."

Humility would say, "Why not me?"

Pride would say, "You don't deserve to die in such a slow, degenerative way."

Humility would say, "Everyone dies. That is just reality. Face death with dignity and choose to be joyful."

That's a recurring conversation I've had with pride and humility!

Before I experienced PD, I worried about what others thought of me and went out of my way to perform for their acceptance and affirmation. What I came to realize is that if people only liked me based on my performance, they did not like me for me! That all changed the day I recognized God loved me despite my performance and that recognition set me free from the need to jump through hoops to gain acceptance and affirmation. Now I perform BECAUSE I am accepted and affirmed and LOVED by my heavenly Father and NOT so I will be.

Still, through the years, I allowed some of the old ways of thinking to creep back into my thought life. As I grew into my 40s, my hair— especially my facial hair— began to gray. Because the music industry exalts youth and youthful appearance, I felt a pull to dress a certain way and to exercise to maintain a youthful and fit appearance, often walking the tightrope between a cool 40-something and an old guy obviously trying to appear young! I even went through a period of dying my beard every other week. That changed when one of my daughters-in-law came to me and asked, "Why do you dye your beard?"

I asked in return, "Is it that obvious?"

Her look said it all. "Duh." Her kind response was, "You don't need to do that. We love you just the way you are."

In that moment, I had to ask myself, "Why am I doing this? Am I trying to 'fix' my appearance to make myself seem more valuable to others? Am I trying to prolong youth?" When I began to ask such honest questions, I was comforted by this truth: Altering my outward appearance does nothing to alter my intrinsic value to God. It does nothing to change the way my children and grandchildren perceive me. This is a pride problem, and pride is beaten by humility.

I am not saying one is prideful or self-focused if they choose to alter their appearance. I just believe that before taking steps to do so one should ask why. A nose job or Botox or liposuction or any manner of cosmetic surgery can be therapeutic, but often, we undergo body-altering procedures that have no therapeutic value at all other than our own vanity. I believe my body is the temple of God's Holy Spirit and base that belief on 1 Peter 3:3-4, which gives us this sobering truth that outward beauty always fades but that real beauty emanates from the inside out. Real beauty is always unfading. The beauty of a gentle and quiet spirit, true beauty, radiates from the inside out.

I recently heard someone describe what real beauty looks like to them, and it caused me to look into my own heart and define what real beauty looks like to me. To me, beauty is found when I look away from the mirror. It's in the smile of a person whose life has been marred by tragedy but radiates God's amazing grace; in a face full of wrinkles brought on by many years of joy and laughter and fiery trials endured; in the contentment of a man with a dad bod who wears it proudly because he feels so beyond satisfied by his adoring wife's cooking; in the twinkle of the eyes of a woman who spends more time with her children than in front of a mirror applying makeup; in the spark of love still evident in an elderly couple walking slowly hand in hand down the lane.

It's in the man whose hands appear to be rough and worn from a hard day's work yet are both strong enough to give his children a bear hug or wrestle with them to the point of exhaustion and sensitive enough to carry them lovingly to bed and tuck them in for the night; in the extra weight put on by that expectant new mother; in the sweatpants-wearing wife who is made to feel beautiful by her husband's frisky gaze; in the raucous laughter of children playing in a mud puddle rather than left alone and silent in front of a cell phone gaming screen; in Melinda and me slow dancing to Ed Sheeran's "Thinking Out Loud" so slowly we are barely moving at all (except for my pesky little tremor)!

There is beauty all around us if we just take the time to look, and it would do us all good if we practiced what God's Word says about the way He sees us. In 1 Samuel 16:7b (NASB), Samuel the prophet says, "God does not see as man sees, since man looks at the outward appearance, but the LORD looks at the heart."

We need to view others from the inside out...and we need to view ourselves in the same way.

I almost titled this chapter "The Beauty of Growing Old" because I am finding out just how beautiful the journey of growing old truly is...or can be.

When my dad was alive, I was still active in sports like tennis and basketball well into my 40s. One day dad overheard me say how sore my body was from the basketball game I played in the day before. He looked at me and said, "You know you're not 18 anymore."

I responded with, "Tell that to my brain. I still think like an 18-year-old most of the time." While it is absolutely fine to think of oneself as having a young, vibrant mind, there comes a time when we must face the truth. As of this writing, I am 65 years old and feeling every bit of it. Honestly…I think like a 65-year-old man! That just means I now view life from the vantage point of one who has lived a long life and is learning to rest in, and even rejoice in, the wisdom I have gained through the adventure of my life. There comes a time when a man realizes he's no longer the warrior or cowboy or hero and accepts the mantle of a sage.

I plan to always keep the wonder of a child. My goal is to keep learning no matter how old I have the privilege to live, but to live my life as fully and joyfully as possible I must think like a man who is 65 years old, who has been married 40+ years, who has nine children, who has 13 grandchildren, and who has Parkinson's. I cannot hold on to youth. It is impossible, but I can embrace my old age and live my life with purpose and joy. It is better to stop lying to myself and get discouraged by the unrealistic place that attacks my mind and live in the truth that I am where and who I am. It's peaceful, joyful, and, dare I say, beautiful.

There's the story that you want to be true and there's the story that is true. To be free, you must surrender what you both want and don't want to be true. You must face reality if you want to live a life of joy and freedom, even as your physical body grows older and weaker by the day.

PARKINSON'S & RECREATION 2

What I want to be true is that I do not have Parkinson's. What IS true is that I have it. What I want to be true is that I could be with my children and grandchildren every day. What IS true is that's not possible due to time and distance and any number of family dynamics.

What I want to be true is that my personal history with SSA was not controversial. What IS true is that my belief that God could give me a new identity and alter my sexual orientation IS controversial. When I accept reality and the love of God, I find the grace to grow old well!

As I was finishing up this chapter, something notable happened, which seems like an appropriate way to end the chapter on growing old. I had just renewed my driver's license. Once I completed the paperwork, I waited around for several minutes to pay for the license and the woman asked me, "Why are you still here?"

I said, "I need to pay for my license."

She looked befuddled and said, "You're all set. Your driver's license is free for you since you're 65 or older and it will be good for the next eight years!"

I laughed and replied, "This is a great day!" I had to wonder to myself in that moment whether that was due to PD or just another sign that I'm getting old!

FOUR
TRUTH VS. REALITY, PT. 1

"Life is not a problem to be solved, but a reality to be experienced."

— SOREN KIERKEGAARD

These wise words echo through the halls of our home. Even though we are choosing to view Parkinson's from God's perspective, doing our best to differentiate between the truth (I have PD) and the reality (God can use it for our good), we must remember that others are involved in this journey with us, each with their own unique point of view.

This point was driven home when I asked our children to share how Parkinson's has affected them and their own little ones. Our daughter, Annē, a mother of four, quickly responded, her letter tinged with a mix of emotions:

"*Honestly, it affects me in different ways at different times. When I first heard the diagnosis, it was hard to accept in some* ways because I didn't want to see you ever as someone with a serious health issue. You're my dad. You're supposed to always be there and be strong and be there for my kids.

"The reality of Parkinson's has been that you are still my dad who is always there and strong—just in different ways. The parts that hit me hard are knowing how much you want to play hard with your grandkids like you did with us kids, but the PD, in a way, has kept you from going as hard as you would like. That and the fact that you are getting old. Sorry. Some of that is also very much age-related in the fact that you played so hard that you now have two new knees and a couple of repaired shoulders, ha!

"It hurts my heart knowing you struggle to say the words you want when you have a brain freeze or to see you try to hide the party hand. My kids talk about you and your party hand like it is just a part of who you are, and they fully accept it, meaning that you love them more when they are with you because your hand shakes.

"It has been hard though at times to not be able to ask you and mom to watch the kids when we might have needed help because I worry about them being too much for you and whether you've had a hard day. Just being honest. There have been days where I'm sad about it and then times where it isn't a big deal at all. In a way I've had to grieve the dreams I had of how you would get to be with my kids as a grandpa. However, the grandpa you have become and is the best grandpa in the world.

"I love how you still make an effort to be there for the kids and the grandkids in creative ways even when it can be hard *for you to be present. I absolutely love that even before the PD diagnosis you had already started leaving a beautiful legacy for your grandkids in the Forest of Bren and the stories born in the realm. That's so special and I love sharing that you have created a whole fantasy world for just you and mom and the grandkids. No one else in the world has a grandpa that has created a whole new reality for their legacy to live through not only their reality but also the imagination.*

"*I absolutely hate PD for robbing you of the dreams you had and your ability to be as present as I know you want to be. I hate how PD has stolen your ability to use your facial expressions like you used to...the smirk and side eyes you'd give us when someone did something stupid or somebody said something funny. I miss that. However, you now have the best poker face ever and can bluff your way out of every game we play!*

"*I love how you make us laugh about everything and always find the humor. I think I get my positive outlook from you. You always told us, 'You can choose your attitude and how you react to situations. You can choose to be happy and see things in a positive light or you can choose to be sad/angry and miserable: It is a choice.'*

"*I love how you haven't let people get you down who say dumb things about PD or tell you 'how sorry they are' that you have PD. You don't see it as a death sentence because the truth is that it isn't! Just another hurdle in the race we call life that you have to either navigate around, jump over, or run through. You do it gracefully. You show us kids and mom every day how to persevere through hard things and keeping a positive attitude really does make a difference. Thank you.*"

Her words resonate with me, a gentle reminder that Parkinson's has not only impacted Melinda and me, but also the loved ones who walk alongside us. It's a reality we must navigate, not as a problem to be solved, but as a journey to be experienced, together.

It hurts my heart to hear her point of view, I admit, my mind tinged with a mix of emotions as I reflect on my daughter Annē's words. She had shared how she witnessed the challenges I face in playing boisterously with my grandchildren, as I had always dreamed of doing. Yet, as she said, "I love how you still make an effort to be there for the kids and the grandkids in creative ways even when it can be hard for you to be present."

One of my major goals with Parkinson's is to not allow it to keep me hidden away, especially during family gatherings. Recently, we had a large group of the children and grandchildren with us for a week before Halloween. There were nine of our thirteen grandchildren present, ranging in age from 6 months to 10 years old, and they all craved my attention.

At first, I felt a sense of anxiety, not due to my tremor or the possibility of my face freezing up, but from feeling overwhelmed with how to make each child feel loved, valued, seen, heard, and special to me. But I was determined to be present and engaged.

From the beginning of that week, I forced myself to sit at the table when the adults were talking, to sit in the room where the children were playing, to teach them how to play "The Knuckle Song" on the piano, to play frisbee, catch, and wrestle with them, to go fishing, carve pumpkins, and even create a scavenger/treasure hunt.

PARKINSON'S & RECREATION 2

And you know what? The anxiety vanished like a puff of smoke in the wind! I found the strength to endure the dreaded moments of Parkinson's fogginess and worked through it. The grandchildren didn't know the difference, and my children made me feel seen and valued, even when they noticed a moment of me stammering to get my next word out. What was actually happening was that I was taking my eyes off myself and my needs and pouring myself into them and theirs... and found my strength being renewed.

That week, I wrote out a plan for a big treasure hunt for the grands. This involved creating three riddles that the older children would help the younger children solve. Melinda and I loaded up in the Gator with the little ones, while the older ones ran ahead of us into the magical Forest of Bren.

The first riddle took them to the campground, where a majestic cedar tree stood, decorated with Christmas ornaments year-round. In Grandma and Grandpa's forest, it is Christmas year-round. The older children helped the younger ones locate the hidden second clue, and one of them read it aloud.

As soon as the clue had been read, they all shouted in unison, "It means the next clue is somewhere near Bigfoot!" Again, the little ones rode with Melinda and me, while the older ones ran ahead. They waited patiently in the vine-covered area of the forest where Bigfoot stood, as we made our way slowly through the winding trails.

As soon as we rolled up, the younger children shouted excitedly, "It's in his arm! It's in his arm!"

Sure enough, the third clue was rolled up and tucked between Bigfoot's side and left arm. Again, an older cousin helped the younger ones by reading the clue and guiding them to the solution. Before Melinda and I could tell them to slow down, they were off to the races, shouting, "It's buried near the alligator! The treasure is near the alligator!"

I could only shout ahead to the older boys, "Do not dig up the treasure until we get there!" and heard the faintest of replies, "We'll wait for you..."

The younger children could hardly keep their seats, freaking out with anticipation, wondering if a treasure truly existed and if they would be able to find and dig it up. This truly did make my soul very happy and complete, even though the Parkinson's, combined with all the physical activities of the past week, had left me almost completely exhausted.

Along with the clue found with Bigfoot, a treasure map had been discovered, complete with an 'X' marking the spot. What I had not told them was that there were actually TWO X's, causing major confusion and wonderful frustration as Melinda and I watched them work together to figure it out. "One 'X' must be a decoy!" said one child, with a bevy of little voices echoing, "Yeah! A decoy!" Taking turns, each child dug a few scoops out of the ground beneath the second 'X' using Melinda's small garden tools, determined to uncover the hidden treasure.

As the children dug deeper, each one seemed to hold their breath in anticipation, the rhythmic scraping of their tools against the earth creating a tense, suspenseful soundtrack. Suddenly, one of the tools clanged against something solid, and at the urging of the older boys, a little one brought his rake down on the object, revealing a hollow, wooden sound.

"We found it! I can see it now! It's a treasure chest! A real-life treasure chest!" they cried out in a chorus of urgency and awe, even the older ones who had "figured it out." With utmost care, they lifted the small wooden box and placed it gently on the ground, slowly unlatching the clasp. As they stood there in awed silence, I asked them to step back, unsure of what we might find. Holding my breath, I slowly lifted the lid.

The small box was brimming with a dazzling array—diamonds of various shapes and sizes, colorful stone "coins," and stunning blue and yellow pieces of real obsidian. I wish you could have heard their collective oohs and aahs, their mouths agape in pure wonder. I then instructed them to take turns, each child allowed to choose one diamond and two pieces of obsidian as their share of the treasure of Bren, for they were all princes and princesses of this realm.

Did it wear me out? Absolutely. Was it worth it? Without a single doubt. Why go to such elaborate lengths, investing so much time and energy? Because I want our grandchildren to know they are worth every moment, every ounce of effort...and to have no doubt of the depth of my love for them.

Was it true? Every word. Was it real? Anything that echoes love, worth, joy, and adventure in the heart and mind of a child is utterly real to that child. I find great joy in knowing such stories will be passed down through the generations, and I anticipate many more fantastic, hard-to-believe memories to be created for those future generations long after I am gone. For you see, I don't believe anyone is ever truly forgotten, as I hold fast to my faith in Jesus Christ and the promise of eternity. I suspect He is waiting for me, even now, planning my next treasure hunt and countless more adventures to come.

FIVE
THE GRANDKIDS

You know, I think it's high time we shook things up a bit in this book, don't you? When it comes to my grandkids, I've got a treasure trove of material that could fill these pages to the brim. Seriously, these little mischief-makers of mine keep me on my toes, and I wouldn't have it any other way.

As Ben Vereen so eloquently put it, "They keep their grandpa informed on what's going on." And the things that come out of their mouths sometimes—it's like they've got a direct line to the fountain of pure, unfiltered wisdom. Don't worry, parents, your secrets are safe with me...unless, of course, they're too good not to share!

Being with my grandkids is like a soothing balm for my Parkinson's-weary soul. Hearing their unique perspectives on life is like a refreshing breeze, washing away the heaviness of my struggles. If Parkinson's is the gift that keeps on taking, as Michael J. Fox says, then my grandchildren are the gifts that keep on giving. And I'll take all the joy and laughter I can get.

Watching them grow up is like an epic fantasy adventure, full of surprises and moments that can bring me to tears, both of laughter and of sincere emotion. I never know what's going to come out of their little mouths next, but I find myself eagerly anticipating the next zinger, the next moment of pure, unadulterated hilarity. It's a wild ride, but I wouldn't trade it for the world.

One of the greatest joys in my life has been raising my nine children with Melinda. It was an absolute treasure, and I consider myself a truly rich man because of it. But as much as I love my kids, I've always tried to strike a careful balance. I don't want to be the dad who's constantly meddling in their own family dynamics, you know? I want them to create their own traditions, their own way of doing things. Don't get me wrong: I'm grateful when they carry on the family customs from their childhoods, but there's something so rewarding about watching them take ownership of their own family identities.

At the same time, I want my children to know that I'm always here for them, that they can count on me to drop everything and be there in a heartbeat. Having that kind of open-door policy helps me keep my Parkinson's in perspective, and it gives me the freedom to write and share without crossing any lines when it comes to their private lives.

Which brings me to the whole reason for this chapter—my grandkids! As a grandpa, I figure I've got free rein to share all sorts of hilarious, heartwarming moments. I mean, these little munchkins of mine keep me in stitches on the regular. Their random quips and unfil-

PARKINSON'S & RECREATION 2

tered perspectives are a constant source of joy and laughter, and that's exactly what I need to stay focused on rather than dwelling on this Parkinson's thing.

I could probably fill an entire book just with the shareable moments from my 13 grandkids, but I'll try to give you a little sampling of the grandchild bliss that keeps me going. Brace yourselves because these kids say the darndest things!

You know, one of the coolest things I've done for my grandkids is creating this actual fantasy forest on our property. We're talking over two miles of winding trails, each one named after one of the little ones. Melinda and I have filled that place with all sorts of magical statues and creatures, and we even keep a Christmas tree decorated year-round because, hey, it's Christmas all the time in the Forest of Bren!

As part of this enchanted wonderland, I've written a whole series of books called "The Bairns of Bren," where my grandkids are the heroes. We've got *Hide and Seek*, *The Light Eater*, and *The Puzzle*—stories that are just perfect for those 9- to 12-year-old readers. And let me tell you, my two eldest grandsons, ages 10 and 9, have devoured those books and come back to me with the most insightful feedback. They've been dropping hints that they want even more heroic parts in the next volumes!

The younger ones have been catching wind of the older kids' excitement, and they're starting to dive into the books too. Just the other day, I got this message from my daughter Hannah in Australia, talking about her 5-year-old, Matilda. Apparently, Tilly's been reading *The Puzzle* at bedtime, just scouring the pages to find everyone's names. Hannah said Tilly thinks she's famous now, and she even sent me these hilarious photos of Tilly posing dramatically, like she's the star of a photoshoot.

That little Aussie whirlwind of energy is the spitting image of her mom, Hannah, but with even more passion and zest for life. And I didn't think that was possible! I swear, it's like watching Hannah 2.0 grow up right before my eyes. The other day, Hannah sent me another Tilly story that just had me in stitches, even with this Parkinson's-frozen face of mine. I can't wait to share it with you!

From Hannah: "The other night, as we were all snuggling up for bedtime, Tilly pipes up, 'Mum, listen! What's that?' And before we could even process what she was talking about, she lets out this big, boisterous fart! The look on her face was priceless—a mix of delight and mischief. And then, to really seal the deal, she turns to me and asks, 'Do you want to smell it?' Needless to say, we were all in stitches!"

Speaking of unexpected surprises, our family chat recently took an interesting turn when the topic of tornadoes came up. Our daughter Hannah was relaying a message from Tilly, who was apparently scarred for life after watching the movie *Twister*. She was adamant that she didn't want to visit America during tornado season, no matter how many storm shelters we had. Hannah tried to assure her that we have top-notch weather alerts and plenty of safe spots, but Matilda was having none of it. That girl's got an anti-tornado zeal that's truly admirable!

And the tornado talk didn't stop there. A few weeks later, Hannah shared the most hilarious story. Apparently, Matilda had been telling random strangers at her band practice pickup that she wants to go back to America, but only when it's not tornado season. And she'd throw in the fact that she's partly American, all while twirling and rolling around like a whirlwind herself! Hannah was in stitches, and I have to say, I'm with her. That girl is the best.

Of course, living in Tornado Alley, we'll have to do our best to convince Matilda that the siren she hears is just the city's way of welcoming her, and then quickly usher her and her family to the basement for a good old-fashioned "playtime." In that same family chat, another of our daughters, Galen, asked Hannah if there were drills in Australia for things we don't have in America. Hannah's response was pure Aussie gold: "Nah, we're all, 'She'll be right, mate.'" That laid-back, joy-filled attitude is truly an inspiration, and it helps me keep my Parkinson's in check.

Our daughter Annē shared the most delightful commentary from our grandson Ronald while he was watching the movie *Battleship*. That boy's got a real knack for film critique—he was just tickled pink, exclaiming "This is just like the game!" and then marveling at the "dark twists and then...boom!" I swear, he's going to give Rotten Tomatoes a run for their money someday.

Ronald's big brother, Cullen, nearing the end of one of the hottest summers on record in Oklahoma, the summer of 2023, had a conversation with his mom. Annē wrote, "Cullen is a child after my own heart. I just told him how excited I am for this cooler weather because it means a good, cool, crisp fall afternoon and he said, 'Oh, yeah! With a crunchy taco by my side!'"

The joys of family life and all the little moments that make our hearts swell with love and laughter do my heart good.

SIX
OF VIKINGS

"Better to fight and fall than to live without hope."

— VOLSUNGA, C.12

"Ill is the result of letting fear rule thine actions."

— THE SAGA OF HARALD HARDRADE, C.46

One of the things I have done to help me step from the autumn of life into the winter of life is to study my family heritage. There is nothing like researching a family tree to help one come to understand a bit more about their own personality and identity. Using a free genealogy website called FamilySearch.com, I have uncovered a rich tapestry of my family's history, tracing my lineage back to the year 1015 AD.

As I delve into the annals of my family's past, I am struck by the resilience and adventurous spirit that seems to flow through the Jernigan bloodline. I have discovered that it was not uncommon for families in my ancestry to have 10 or more children. Ah, now I understand the source of my own innate desire for a large family. It was quite literally in my genes all along!

But the most intriguing revelation from my family history research is the discovery of my Viking heritage. Yes, Norse blood courses through the Jernigan veins. I can almost hear the battle cries of my ancestors, the roar of longships cutting through the choppy seas, the clink of swords and the crackle of burning thatched roofs in small English villages. Of course, these are the "dark days" of our family history, as I now refer to them, but they are no less a part of who I am.

I have traced my family's lineage to a famous Danish king named Heremod, born in 1015 AD in what is now present-day Denmark. This legendary figure, both king of the Danes and the Angles, has been immortalized in the Old English poem Beowulf, where a bard sings of the deeds of Sigmund:

> "He had of all heroes the highest renown among races of men, this refuge-of-warriors, for deeds of daring that decked his name since the hand and heart of Heremod grew slack in battle. He, swiftly banished to join with Jutes at mercy of foes, to death was betrayed; for torrents of sorrow had lamed him too long; a load of care to earls and athelings all he proved. Oft indeed, in earlier days, for the warrior's wayfaring wise men mourned, who had hoped of him help from harm and bale, and had thought their sovran's son would thrive, follow his father, his folk protect, the hoard and the stronghold, heroes' land, home of Scyldings."

PARKINSON'S & RECREATION 2

It appears that Heremod, my illustrious ancestor, was banished by his own subjects and forced to flee to the Jutes, where he was betrayed and met his demise. This dark chapter in our family's history is recounted in the immortal verses of Beowulf, where after Beowulf has slain Grendel's dam, King Hrothgar speaks again of Heremod:

"I have heard the tale of Heremod
How the ale-warriors' joy was ended
His might and his mind-thoughts
Became turned to evil,
He was betrayed to his foes."

"Was not Heremod thus to offspring of Ecgwela, Honor-Scyldings, nor grew for their grace, but for grisly slaughter, for doom of death to the Danishmen. He slew, wrath-swollen, his shoulder-comrades, companions at board! So he passed alone, chieftain haughty, from human cheer. Though him the Maker with might endowed, delights of power, and uplifted high above all men, yet blood-fierce his mind, his breast-hoard, grew, no bracelets gave he to Danes as was due; he endured all joyless strain of struggle and stress of woe, long feud with his folk."

— BEOWULF

Ain't that a kick in the pants?! One minute a revered king, the next cast out and betrayed to his death. And I thought dealing with Parkinson's on an off day was rough. The twists and turns of my ancestor Heremod's life read like the pages of a Shakespearean tragedy.

As I delve deeper into the tapestry of my family's past, the threads of Heremod's story become ever more vivid. This legendary figure's reign was short-lived, for he was ultimately banished by his own subjects, forced to flee to the Jutes, where he met his demise at the hands of those with whom he sought refuge.

Heremod's fall from grace serves as a stark reminder of the consequences of succumbing to fear and losing one's way. Yet, even in the darkest of moments, a glimmer of hope shines through, for as the old Norse saying goes, "Better to fight and fall than to live without hope."

Interestingly, the name "Jernigan" itself appears to hold great significance. Heremod's son, Scoland, also known as Scoland Jernegan, King of Denmark and Scotland, seems to mark the beginning of our family's transition from Viking raiders to kings in their own right. Perhaps it was Scoland, or one of his descendants, who began to temper the family's penchant for plunder and pillage, ushering in a new era of stability and leadership.

As I ponder the twists and turns of my family's history, I am struck by the depth of meaning that can be found in a single name. "What's in a name?" Shakespeare once mused. In the case of the Jernigans, it would appear that the name itself carries the weight of a storied past, a testament to the resilience and adaptability of our ancestors.

The tale of my family's lineage is intertwined with the rise and reign of the mighty Danish king, Canute. In 1016 AD, this formidable prince ascended the throne of England, later adding the crowns of Denmark and Norway to his domain, forging what was known as the North Sea Empire. It was during Canute's illustrious rule that the Jernigan clan found favor, their military service and unwavering loyalty earning them the respect and gratitude of the king himself.

As Canute's North Sea Empire flourished, he bestowed upon my ancestors titles of nobility and granted them manors and estates, cementing their place as a prominent family in the annals of history. This legacy of land ownership resonates deeply with me, for as the protagonist Delmar O'Donnell so eloquently put it in the Coen brothers' classic film, *O Brother, Where Art Thou?*, "You ain't no kind of man if you ain't got land."

Looking back on our family lineage, I can see that owning land is the equivalent of having one's own small kingdom, which then makes me recall the phrase "a man's home is his castle." Melinda and I, a few years into our own marriage, made the decision to acquire a 113-acre parcel, our goal being to bequeath a 10-acre allotment to each of our children. But this land represents more than just a material possession–it is a sanctuary, a refuge, and a wellspring of dreams and visions for the generations to come.

As I pen our lineage, I am mindful that this work serves not merely as a historical account, but as an allegorical guide—a means of instilling in our descendants the understanding that, no matter the circumstances they face, they have the power to choose how they respond. For even as some urge me to slow down and rest on my laurels, I am driven by the conviction that there is still work to be done, legacies to be forged, and a godly, positive perspective to impart.

Even as I pour my heart and soul into this family mythology, I find myself met with well-meaning suggestions to slow down and coast into the twilight of my days. "You've earned the right to rest," they say. I'll be darned if I let that stop me from forging ahead.

Just because I've reached the golden years and contend with the challenges of Parkinson's doesn't mean I'm ready to wave the white flag. Nay, I feel the call to loot and pillage, to ransack the very depths of my creativity and wrest control from the grip of this debilitating disease. Parkinson's may show me no mercy, but I'll be thrice damned if I show it an ounce of quarter. I intend to pillage the harsh realities of life, extracting the good and the joy that can be found in the divine perspective.

For I am consumed by the knowledge that my Heavenly Father can take even the most dreadful of circumstances and use them for my good. That makes me a conqueror, for He has conquered even death on my behalf. I've always been a Viking at heart, in pursuit of walking in victory over my circumstances.

Being a Viking with the heart of a warrior is a legacy I wish to impart to my children and grandchildren. So, if you'll excuse me, I suddenly have a craving for a Danish pastry—a taste of my ancestral heritage, a reminder that the spirit of the Norsemen still burns bright within me.

SEVEN
DOWN UNDER?

"Australians don't have a preconceived notion of what things have to be...we can go on a fantastic journey."

— YAHOO SERIOUS

"It is better to travel well than to arrive."

— BUDDHA

"Wherever you go, go with all your heart."

— CONFUCIUS

One of our daughters, Hannah, ventured off to college in Sydney, Australia, where she crossed paths with the man who would later become her husband, Ashley Brown, or simply, Ash. They now have two remarkable daughters and lead a wonderful life down under. The only downside is that we don't get to spend as much time with them in person as any of us would wish. While video chats help bridge the distance, they can never quite replace the warmth of a hug, the comfort of holding hands, or the simple joy of sharing a quiet moment on the back deck.

I've had the opportunity to visit Australia thrice in the past 15 years, while Melinda has been fortunate to make the journey five times. When I received my PD diagnosis, we knew my days of extensive travel for public engagements were behind me. This realization also stirred a pang of sorrow at the thought of potentially never being able to visit my beloved daughter, exceptional son-in-law, and stunning granddaughters in their Australian abode.

Two years ago, a delightful turn of events led them to spend three weeks with us in our home. Despite it being the peak of summer, we embarked on numerous escapades in the enchanting Forest of Bren, indulged in daily swims, and even hosted a few illicit bonfires around which I and a dozen of our grandchildren danced like wild spirits for hours on end.

Our Aussie granddaughters had never encountered fireflies, which we fondly call lightning bugs in Oklahoma. I'll forever cherish the moment when one of their aunts, Glory, demonstrated how to extract the glowing abdomens from the fireflies and fashion them into glow-in-the-dark earrings for the girls' earlobes! Perhaps a tad mischievous? Definitely. Uncommon? Absolutely delightful! At the time, Elliott and Matilda were 8 and 5, respectively. The memories we crafted during that period are like soul-nourishing sustenance that could sustain me for eternity.

PARKINSON'S & RECREATION 2

As the time approached for my Australian family to return home, none of us were eager to part ways. The farewell at the airport proved to be one of the most heart-wrenching moments I've ever faced, until the looming question surfaced, "Will G Pa (the endearing title bestowed upon me by my Aussie granddaughters) ever be able to journey to visit us in our homeland?"

Initially, a wave of desolation washed over me as I pondered, *Realistically, do I possess the stamina to embark on such a lengthy voyage?* This question marked the toughest challenge I've encountered since my diagnosis.

The subsequent year found me grappling with this quandary persistently. My children had expended significant resources to grace us with their presence, a gesture of immense sacrifice. This prompted me to contemplate, *What sacrifices would I be willing to make in order to reunite with my Australian kin and share moments in their homeland?* Broaching the topic of a potential visit stirred a flurry of reservations in Melinda, who foresaw the arduous nature of such an excursion, not solely in physical terms but also in the emotional and mental toll it could exact. Her concerns were valid, given her pivotal role as my primary caregiver, and truth be told, I witness the toll it occasionally inflicts on her spirit as she ensures my well-being and needs are well attended.

During my 2023 neurologist check-up, I received an uplifting health report that sparked a glimmer of hope. Buoyed by this positive assessment, I seized the moment to pose the pivotal question to my neurologist, "Do you believe I am sufficiently fit to journey to Australia and spend time with our family there?"

Without hesitation, he reassured me, "You are free to travel anywhere in the world you desire! You'll do just fine!"

In a nutshell, Melinda took charge and secured our tickets for a January 2024 voyage, but as luck would have it, things promptly started unraveling—classic! My wrists were escalating into a real hassle, impeding even the simplest of tasks requiring hand dexterity. Turning a doorknob morphed into a Herculean feat at times. To compound matters, a left hip mishap added a fresh layer of discomfort, rendering vehicle entries and exits excruciating, donning underwear and pants a daily ordeal, and the race to sock up in under two minutes a true test of mettle. Such is the rollercoaster ride of navigating life with PD or perhaps, just perhaps, a gentle nudge from the universe reminding me of the inevitable march of time, haha!

To add to the chaos, my trusted office manager of 28 years, Trish, bid adieu, effective December 31, 2023, without the chance for a proper sendoff due to scheduling conflicts. As if that wasn't enough, my mother, Peggy, who had dedicated 22 years to working alongside me, also chose to retire, commencing January 31, 2023. This double blow struck a chord deep within me that words fail to capture adequately. Trish had poured her heart into supporting me and my ministry, and not being able to bid her a proper farewell left me with a heavy heart. The final week of December 2023 was steeped in melancholy, especially considering our impending trip slated for January 1-27, 2024.

PARKINSON'S & RECREATION 2

As I wallowed in self-pity during that final week of December, I sought solace in my studio, my man cave, engrossed in writing to distract my mind from the lingering sadness. With my staff on holiday break, I assumed I was in solitary company. The creak of the barn door opening initially led me to believe it was Melinda, but a knock on my studio door swiftly dispelled that notion. Melinda would have barged in without a second thought.

Unsure of who waited on the other side, I uttered a hesitant, "Come in." A wave of relief washed over me the moment I laid eyes on the visitor—it was Trish! She had come to bid me farewell before our trip, rueful for not having the chance to do so earlier. Overwhelmed with emotion, I embraced her, professing, "You have no need to apologize! Thank you for your unwavering support over the years. For your grace in representing me. For your integral role in the success of my ministry. I deeply regret the lack of a proper sendoff. Let's plan something, a luncheon or dinner, in the upcoming year. Your visit means more to me than words can express."

This simple yet profound gesture sparked a shift in my perspective, filling me with anticipation and optimism as we geared up for the flight across the vast Pacific Ocean in the following week. But hold on, there's more! While meticulously curating creative content for my Patreon page and scheduling posts to engage my Patreon team, disaster struck. My studio computer breathed its last! A sinking feeling gripped my heart as I grappled with the realization that nearly 35 years of creative work resided in that now-defunct machine, the extent of its backup uncertain. Moreover, my beloved podcast relied on that very computer for recording and production. Thankfully, I had pre-recorded 16 weeks' worth of podcasts to alleviate any recording concerns during my upcoming journey.

Coming to terms with letting go of my need for control felt like a futile battle. There was little else I could do but surrender to the belief that God orchestrates everything for my benefit and his glory. Recalling the advice I've imparted to others over the years, I embraced the concept of yielding control and releasing my insistence on things going my way, entrusting it all to God. It truly boiled down to that simple act of surrender. Living with Parkinson's has required me to navigate this process daily, at times even moment by moment. Redirecting my focus toward my wife and family in Australia, I made a conscious choice to find happiness amidst the chaos. This shift in mindset not only lifted my spirits but also filled me with genuine anticipation for the days ahead. Now, let me regale you with tales of our trip.

As previously mentioned, grappling with the progression of Parkinson's, persistent hip discomfort, and the challenges of carpal tunnel syndrome affecting multiple fingers on each hand left me uncertain about embarking on the journey to Sydney, Australia, to reunite with our daughter and her family for the entirety of January 2024.

However, a game changer emerged in the form of wheelchair assistance available at every gate, offering us invaluable support and the added perk of being among the first to board the plane at each juncture.

PARKINSON'S & RECREATION 2

Stepping onto each flight, the observant flight attendants stationed to greet passengers at the entrance quickly noticed my struggle with walking and kindly extended a helping hand. "Thank you for the assistance, but I'm managing with Parkinson's," I'd say, and a shift would occur—their voices softened, drawing nearer to my ear, and their words became more deliberate, as if speaking to someone hard of hearing. Initially taken aback, I soon realized this was their way of displaying compassion.

I felt a tinge of embarrassment at first, yet I had to embrace the fact that my challenges were evident to all, prompting me to accept their gestures of kindness, even if it meant feeling a bit self-conscious. It's one thing for your family to be privy to your struggles and vulnerabilities and quite another to navigate these moments with strangers encountered during lengthy 15-hour flights across the Pacific Ocean. I also found the change in attitude and vocal tone immensely hilarious because I did not feel helpless at all, but did I refuse the extra help and attention? Are you out of your mind? I ate it up!

Upon our arrival in Sydney, the wheelchair experience took on a whole new level of cool. Settling into the motorized wheelchair steered by an airport hospitality assistant from behind, I couldn't help but draw a contrast. Older wheelchairs felt akin to the old Conestoga wagons ferrying families and belongings across the American frontier in pioneer days, while this new chair seemed more like the Millennium Falcon from Star Wars!

Thanks to my wheelchair-bound status, we effortlessly glided through customs, emerging into the terminal where I felt regal, perched on my mobile throne as I was whisked away to reunite with our eagerly awaiting family. Prior to catching sight of them, I raised my hand and began a royal wave, envisioning myself as a monarch parading through adoring crowds. Anticipating the delight it would bring our granddaughters, who revel in their connection to the British Commonwealth of Nations, I could already hear their laughter echoing. Elliott and Matilda rushed into our open arms, their laughter mingling with our tears, creating a heartwarming tableau and a grand entrance fit for royalty. Just another unexpected perk courtesy of Parkinson's.

EIGHT
OF ENGLISH NOBILITY

The noble lineage of the Jernigan family can be traced back through the ages. The very definition of nobility—"having or showing fine personal qualities or high moral principles and ideals"—rings true in the rich history of this illustrious clan.

As I've delved into the Jernigan family tree, I've uncovered a fascinating journey from Viking roots to English nobility and ultimately to the status of good old-fashioned American blue collar folk. The Jernegan name first emerged in Scotland, later being Anglicized after 1035 AD. Over the course of 18 generations spanning 579 years, the name evolved, taking on various forms such as Jerningham, FitzJernigan, and Fitzhugh Jernegan—the "Fitz" and "Fitzhugh" prefixes meaning "son of" and "son of Hugh," respectively.

The Jernigans' eventual transition to the New World is a bit of a mystery, but one name in the family tree stands out as the likely trailblazer: Sir Thomas "The Immigrant" Jernigan, who lived from 1614 to 1668. While the specifics of his journey and where he settled are unclear, his moniker alone speaks volumes about his pivotal role in bringing the Jernigan legacy to America.

Delving deeper into the Jernigan family history, the records reveal that the illustrious Sir Thomas made his way to the New World in 1635, settling in the village of Nansemond in the British colony of Virginia. This intrepid ancestor was later granted land at Somerton, Virginia, in 1668. Interestingly, many of his descendants went on to become seasoned sea captains, with his son Thomas even establishing a homestead on Martha's Vineyard, Massachusetts, in 1712.

Sir Thomas' occupational journey is quite fascinating; he started out as a mariner, but later transitioned into the role of tax collector for King Charles I. This tidbit certainly explains my love of scuba diving and aversion to the IRS! It's worth noting that Charles I's reign was cut short when he became the first British monarch to be executed, with his head being lopped off in front of the Banqueting House in Whitehall. One can only hope that Sir Thomas "The Immigrant" was not responsible for any clerical errors that contributed to this untimely demise!

Delving even further back into the family tree, I have uncovered the occupations of several other distinguished Jernigan ancestors. The grandfather of Sir Thomas "The Immigrant," also named Thomas Jernigan, served as a representative in the English Parliament and resided with his family in Stebbing, Essex. Earlier still, Thomas' father, George Jerningham, held the esteemed position of Chancel (likely a bishop's law officer) in the picturesque town of Somerleyton, Suffolk, where he made his home.

The family's royal connections don't end there, as my research reveals that Sir Knight John Jerningham, the father of George Jerningham, served the royal court of England during the reigns of several monarchs, including King Henry VII, King Henry VIII, King Edward VI, Queen Mary I, and possibly even Queen Elizabeth I. It is believed that Sir Knight John was in charge of the royal stables.

The Jernigan family's noble lineage continues to impress, as my research has uncovered the captivating life of Sir Edward Jerningham, the father of Sir Knight John Jerningham. Sir Edward was a devout Catholic, which may help explain the family's apparent propensity for prolific procreation (wink, wink).

On May 11, 1509, Sir Edward had the distinct honor of serving as a gentleman usher at the funeral of King Henry VII. He must have made quite an impression, as he was then retained in service to the new monarch, King Henry VIII. Sir Edward's official title was Gentleman Usher of the King's Chamber, which begs the question: Was he tasked with ushering in the king's, shall we say, "guests" (mistresses)? Or perhaps he was in charge of the royal chamber pot? The mind reels at the possibilities!

Adding to his impressive resume, on June 24, 1509, Sir Edward was assigned the prestigious role of chief cupbearer at the coronation of Catherine of Aragon, the wife of King Henry VIII. Sir Edward and his wife, Margaret Bedingfeld, made their home in Somerleyton, where they were both laid to rest at Saint Mary's Catholic Church.

Diving even deeper into the family's rich history, I have uncovered details about Sir Edward's father, Sir

John Jernegan, who was born in 1430 and lived in Somerleyton. Sir John's father, John Jernegan, was born in 1410 and held the noble title of Knight of the realm. John Jernegan's father, Sir Thomas Jernegan, was born in 1380, passed away in 1450, and was buried in the historic county of Caernarfonshire, Wales. The family's Welsh roots run deep, as Sir Thomas' father, John Jernegan III, was born in 1353 and met his demise in 1401 at the grand Gwydir Castle in Conwy, Wales. And finally, John Jernegan III's father, Sir John Jernegan II, was born in 1325 and died in 1375.

Buckle up, folks, because the story of John Jernegan I reads like a medieval soap opera straight out of the hit TV series, Dynasty! This ancestor's life was nothing short of a whirlwind of matrimonial adventures.

Let's dive into the details, shall we? Records show that John Jernegan I first married a woman named Matilda, who was the daughter and heiress of Sir Roger de Herling of Herling in Norfolk. Now, if you're scratching your head over that heraldic jargon, let me break it down for you. The Herling coat of arms featured a silver (or "argent") background with a rearing black ("sable") unicorn. Quite the regal emblem, if I do say so myself!

The genealogical record also indicates that John Jernegan at some point took a second wife, Isabell, who was the daughter and heiress of a Sir Jervace. This is evidenced by the Jernegan family's coat of arms, which can be seen adorning the walls of Horham Church, put there by none other than Sir John Jernegan himself.

And the plot thickens! John Jernegan I's third wife was Agatha, the daughter of Sir Robert Shelton of Shelton in Norfolk. This marriage produced a son, Sir John Jernegan II, who would go on to inherit the Fitz Osbert estates upon the death of his cousin, Sir John Noyoun. Sir John Jernegan II then married Joan, the daughter and co-heir of Sir William de Kelvedon, and the widow of Sir John Lowdham of Frenze, also in Norfolk. Phew, that's a lot of marriage and inheritance to keep track of!

The saga continues, as Sir John Jernegan II's son, Sir John Jernegan III, married Margaret, the daughter of Sir Thomas Vis de Lou of Shotley, in 1374. This union was cemented by Sir John Jernegan II, who settled the manor and advowson (church patronage) of Stonham Jernegan and Horham Jernegan upon the newlyweds and their heirs.

Truly, the Jernegan family tree reads like a Shakespearean drama, complete with royal connections, inheritances, and enough marital intrigue to rival even the most scandalous of soap operas. Sit back, relax, and enjoy the show, dear readers!

Peter Jernegan (1288-1346) was a knight and sub-escheator of Suffolk, AKA the property whisperer. Yep, his gig was all about making sure lands reverted to the big bosses when heirs were MIA. Talk about a real estate power move! And—wait for it—he also moonlighted as a coroner. Talk about a side hustle! The Jernegan clan sure knows how to keep things interesting. One of my brothers even rocks the funeral home director title in the present, keeping it in the family!

Now, let's rewind a bit. Peter's dad, Walter Jernegan (1250-1299), kept the landowning tradition strong. His father, Sir Hugh Jernigan of Horham (1230-1272), even ended up in a legal tussle with his own mom over some prime real estate. Land squabbles—a true family pastime! Now, Sir Hugh's father, Hubert Jernegan (1177-1239), was another knight in shining armor. Talk about a royal lineage! And then we meet the patriarch, Hugh FitzJernigan (1140-1203), a big shot listed in the 13th century "Red Book of the Exchequer." This guy wasn't just about lands and titles; he was spreading the wealth and making moves for the greater good. Who knew medieval history could be this juicy, right?

And now, cue "The Baronetage of England: Or The History of the English Baronets, Volume 1" by William Betham, bringing all the noble vibes from the reigns of King Stephen and King Henry II. Let the royal saga continue!

If you can stand a bit more history of my family line, you will find a historical treasure trove of the Jernegan legacy! Our story continues with Jernegan, a witness extraordinaire in the Castle Acre Register. Think of him as the document signer, making moves without even a date stamp. And then there's Bryan, son of Scolland, sealing the deal on church confirmations, all the while racking up some serious Exchequer points. Talk about medieval perks!

His son, the one and only Hubert Fitz Jernegan, steps into the spotlight. And according to the legendary Weaver, the Jerningham name has been causing a stir since pre-Conquest days. Legends have it that Canute, the king of Denmark and England, was all about these folks. Can you imagine being a modern-day Dennis Jenihingo? Now that's a name to reckon with! And here's a fun thought: Imagine introducing yourself as Dennis Jenihingo. Pure gold!

Fast forward to the royal decree at Oxford: King Canute ain't playin' around. The Jerninghams snagged some prime Norfolk manors, while the Jennings' scored seaside estates near Harwich. Talk about royal real estate rewards!

Now, let's flip the pages to "Genealogical and Heraldic Dictionary of the Peerage and Baronetage of the British Empire: Burke's Peerage Limited." Brace yourself for a rollercoaster ride through history! The Jernigans have been making waves since Prince Bryan's Denmark departure in 1020. Can you picture the scene as he weds Sabilla, kickstarting the Jernigan dynasty just north of London? From lords to ministers of state, this clan has had their hands in all the pies for centuries. It's like a medieval soap opera, but with more knights and fewer dragons!

Diving deep into my family archives is like uncovering a real-life Game of Thrones plot, complete with coroners and tax collectors. Gotta love those unexpected twists in the family tree!

And speaking of twists, let's fast forward to the Jernigan migration saga to America. It all started with the legendary Sir Thomas "The Immigrant" Jernigan, paving the way for our epic journey across the pond to the land of opportunity—America!

From the Carolinas to Mississippi, our roots spread far and wide. But the real star of the show? My grandpa, Samuel Washington Jernigan, a true World War I hero. Picture this: riding into battle in France on horseback, with those iconic U.S. symbols gleaming on his trusty steed's bridle. Talk about a cinematic family legacy! And that heirloom— those bits from his horse's bridle? They're not just trinkets; they're a piece of history, a connection to my brave ancestor's past. They hold a special place in my heart.

Before World War I, my grandpa embarked on a cross-country horse ride from Mississippi to Oklahoma. Talk about a wild adventure! From the heart of the Muscogee (Creek) nation to the quaint corners of Coal Pool, he made his mark before settling near my childhood stomping grounds in Boynton.

Remembering those who shaped my story is like soul therapy, a balm for the heart. It's a testament to resilience and legacy, echoing through generations. And now, for the grand finale—an excerpt from my book "Parkinson's & Recreation: One Man's Journey Through Parkinson's... So far." It's like a sneak peek into my world, a personal journey of triumph and tenacity:

"I recently had a conversation with one of my 8-year-old grandsons. He came over after school and I was reclining in my chair. When he finds me like that, he always sits right next to me in my chair, snuggling as close as he can get. I asked him how school had gone that day and if there had been any exciting things happen during the course of his day...and he asked me questions in return, wanting to know how my day had gone. I told him, 'My day was made perfect the moment you sat down beside me.'

"His next question caught me off guard and made me quite emotional. He asked, 'What was your grandpa like?' I told him

I had no real memories of my grandpa Jernigan since he had died when I was only 14 months old...but that I felt very loved by him and that he was very proud of me.

"My grandson asked, 'How do you know that if you don't have any memories of him?' In that moment, I had the most tender feelings of bittersweet joy flood through my entire being as I tried to explain to my own grandson why I loved my grandpa so much even though I had no real memories of him. I told him I had actually been told stories of him and me by my grandma Jernigan as I grew older.

"When I was a baby, my grandpa was in his late 60s and he worked as an oil and gas lease pumper or caretaker. His job was to go around to all the various oil and gas lease pumps in his area that covered parts of Okmulgee and and Muskogee counties in northeastern Oklahoma and make sure all the pumps were working and that all the tanks were being tended to.

"Believe it or not, I began walking when I was only 8 months old. By the time I could sit up by myself, my grandpa would come and get me once or twice a week and take me with him to check on his pumps. There were no seatbelts involved. No car seats. He just plopped me down next to him in the seat of his old pickup truck and went about his work. If someone else happened to be at one of the pump sites, my grandpa would take me out of the truck and walk up to the worker and tell him, 'Meet my grandson!'

"My grandma said he would show me off to anyone who would listen. She told me how he would pull his truck off the side of the road if he saw one of his friends working on a fence line and show me off...how he would run into town to fill up *the gas tank on his pickup just so he could show me off to anyone he could. My grandpa loved me so much and was so proud to have me as his grandson that he would take me with him any time he could...just because he could. Even though I have no real memories of my grandpa Jernigan, I have a treasure trove of memories thanks to the stories my grandma told me about him. I will never forget him.*

"My grandson, sounding very wistful and mature beyond his years, then melted my heart beyond what I can adequately describe when he said, 'I will never forget you, Grandpa...'

"No one wants to be forgotten, but time has a way of making us feel we will be one day. Grandchildren have a way of making a grandparent—even one who is dying—feel they will be remembered forever. It is in the passing down of the love of a grandparent to the heart of a child that sees to it that, even though names may be relegated to a place on the family tree, the essence of who we are will never be forgotten."

From the noble Viking roots to its centuries of service to English nobility and the rugged American spirit, the Jernigan family's story is one of enduring strength, resilience, and a steadfast commitment to the ideals of nobility—a legacy that continues to this day.

NINE
A FAMILY AFFAIR

I could not endure the roller coaster ride that is Parkinson's if not for my family. Though our children are grown and out of the home, we stay closely connected. And that is life to me. When I have a rough day, I have a treasure trove of memories to draw upon that lifts me over rough seas. The memory bank is so chock full of family lore—I can easily and instantly make withdrawals. Each one leads me to gratitude and joy.

One of the deliberate endeavors we embarked on when our kids were young were our family trips. Given my nationwide music ministry, it made perfect sense to bring my family along whenever feasible. Countless family anecdotes sprouted from our numerous ski adventures, especially a memorable trip to Breckenridge, Colorado. What made that excursion truly unforgettable were the friendships we forged there—and a particular hat shop that still brings a smile to my face!

For years, our children eagerly anticipated our visits to Breckenridge not just for the skiing, but for a beloved pizza joint and, most notably, the quirky hat emporium I mentioned earlier. We would spend what felt like hours trying on an endless array of hats, ranging from practical cold-weather gear to the zaniest cartoon and superhero-inspired headgear imaginable. The shop didn't just stop at hats; it also boasted magnetic earrings, nose rings, and even fake cigarettes that emitted faux smoke when "puffed." Egged on by my children, I humorously indulged in a fake earring and nose ring, along with a pack of the novelty cigarettes. This lighthearted gesture elicited uproarious laughter, with several of them joining in on the fun by getting their own faux piercings and cigarettes. It was a moment of pure joy and connection that we fondly recall to this day.

After our whimsical hat shop escapade, adorned with our playful faux piercings and fake cigarettes, our merry band paraded down the bustling main street of Breckenridge, unleashing a cacophony of laughter and joy that reverberated through the town. This uproarious moment is etched in my memory, especially the unexpected encounter awaiting us as we strolled along that memorable street.

Given my modest recognition in Christian circles, courtesy of my music, our conspicuous group of eleven, complete with our faux accessories, drew attention. Little did I anticipate the amusing turn of events that was about to unfold.

Amid our raucous revelry, a small cluster of individuals halted our boisterous procession, inquiring, "Aren't you Dennis Jernigan? The Christian singer?" Picture me, with a fake cigarette dangling from my lips and a faux

PARKINSON'S & RECREATION 2

nose piercing adorning my schnoz, caught in a comical yet slightly mortifying moment, attempting to contain my amusement as my children struggled to suppress their giggles.

With a sheepish grin, I removed the prop cigarette and confirmed my identity, admitting, "Yes... I am Dennis Jernigan, the Christian singer. We're just having a bit of fun as a family."

To my surprise, their response was delightful: "We're from Alabama and adore your music! We'll be attending your concert on Sunday evening. Could we snap a photo with you and your family?" I should've quipped about allowing me to finish my "cigarette," but alas, I missed the opportunity for a perfect punchline!

In addition to our family adventures, I made it a priority to take each child on individual trips throughout the year, aligning with my concert commitments. Ski excursions often doubled as quality time with my sons, while special father-daughter date nights became cherished traditions with my girls. Of course, Melinda and I carved out a sacred weekly date night ritual, not only to model a healthy marital bond for our children but also to relish the simple joy of just being regular adults separate from our roles as parents to our brood of nine, haha!

I am reminded of another cherished experience with my children. When they were small, we enjoyed watching the movie *Paulie* about a parrot who could converse with humans. One of the standout lines from the movie, at least to our family, is spoken by the character named Ignacio (a street taco vendor), played by Cheech Marin. While Paulie carries on a conversation with Ignacio,

Paulie, who is on a journey to find his original owner, asks the taco vendor, "Can you tell me where I am?"

Ignacio asks, "You can talk?"

Paulie responds while motioning toward two ordinary parrots perched on the taco cart, "They talk."

Ignacio, in amazement, says, "Them? They don't talk! I say taco! They say 'taco,'" at which time, the two ordinary parrots repeat, "Taco! Taco! Taco!"

Paulie then asks, "Are they OK?"

Why is that one of our favorite lines, you may be asking? It is because, after watching the movie, I could speak the phrase, "I say taco! You say taco!" and my children, all nine of them in unison, would respond with, "Taco! Taco! Taco!" anywhere, anytime, anyplace. I can still utter that phrase to this day and my now-adult children, at least a few of them, still respond with "Taco! Taco! Taco!" much to the amazement of their own children. Such little precious memories help me forget I have Parkinson's sometimes.

TEN
IS LIFE FAIR?

"Life isn't fair, it's just fairer than death, that's all."

— WILLIAM GOLDMAN, *THE PRINCESS BRIDE*

The goal of this book? To give you a fresh perspective on life, sprinkled with a dash of honesty. Let's face it: Life isn't all sunshine and rainbows. It's a rollercoaster of physical, emotional, mental, and relational hurdles. Sorrow and suffering? They've got a front-row seat in life's theater. Sometimes, fairness seems like a distant dream, right?

But hold up...what is fairness? It's like the misunderstood cousin of freedom. Picture this: freedom with guardrails. Like when I watch over my grandkids, if I let them loose on a busy highway, that's not freedom, that's just asking for trouble. So, rules are like the safety net for freedom, keeping us in check.

Oh, and about taking a leap of faith, literally: I once skydived to taste the thrill of soaring through the skies.

Imagine if I ditched the parachute for a "more free" experience. Yeah, not a smart move. Boundaries like that parachute? They're not chains; they're your safety net, your ticket to true freedom.

Fairness, at its core? It's about playing by the same rules— whether in a board game or society. Laws keep us in line, ensuring a level playing field. Justice, impartiality, equality—that's the essence of fairness. But here's the plot twist: Fairness isn't about getting an equal slice of the pie; it's about playing by the same rules, not demanding the same rewards.

In today's world, fairness often gets misused. It's like a magic word for entitlement, a shield to mask self-centered desires. So, next time someone cries "fairness," take a closer look. It might just be a cover-up for a sense of entitlement.

Fairness, huh? Let's break it down with a pinch of humor. Imagine this: a kiddo is playing with a toy, and another one swoops in, demanding to play with it. Classic kid move, right? The toy holder's comeback? "Hey, it's mine for now. Once I'm done, it's all yours. Sharing is caring, but I call the shots." Now, that's fairness in action!

Now, picture me tickling the ivories on my piano. Someone strolls up, eyeing my keys and declares, "You've had your turn. It's my time to shine now."

My response? "This piano's mine, buddy. I'll gladly share once I'm done serenading it." Fair play, right?

Parkinson's, well, it's my sidekick now. Fair or not, it's part of my story. Crying "unfair" would be like wishing this on everyone else. Nope, I'll take the high road. Having Parkinson's is part of life's wild card game—it can hit anyone, anytime. No VIP pass here, just the reality check of life's unpredictability. Rain falls on saints and sinners alike, after all.

God's Word talks about fairness in the following manner:

> "But I say to you, love your enemies and pray for those who persecute you, so that you may prove yourselves to be sons of your Father who is in heaven; for He causes His sun to rise on [the] evil and [the] good, and sends rain on [the] righteous and [the] unrighteous."
>
> — MATTHEW 5:44-45 (NASB)

Let's sprinkle some wisdom and wit on the topic of fairness and freedom. Picture this: God's master plan, where nothing goes to waste, fair or not in our eyes. Instead of the classic "why me?" dance, I ask, "Why NOT me?" God's got this, using even life's curveballs to weave good into my story. That's true freedom right there!

Fairness, now that's a straightforward gig. Imagine a world where everyone pulls their weight, plays by the same rules. No entitlement hangover, no self-imposed chains dragging along. It's all about breaking free from that victimhood trap.

Freedom, for me, is dancing through life hand in hand with a loving God Who turns life's lemons into lemonade. I'm all in for that kind of freedom—no time for fretting over life's fairness score. Fair to say? Pun totally intended!

Life's unfair punches sting, no doubt. But here's the kicker: The real deal lies in what my Heavenly Father says about me. Shifting my perspective on the past flips the script on my feelings. Even the toughest chapters are all part of the grand plan, shaping my story in the long haul.

> "Do not call to mind the former things,
> Or consider things of the past.
> Behold, I am going to do something new,
> Now it will spring up;
> Will you not be aware of it?
> I will even make a roadway in the wilderness,
> Rivers in the desert."
>
> — ISAIAH 43:18-19 (NASB)

Life throws curveballs, right? But we can't let that lead us into the rabbit hole of entitlement. Truth bomb: Our awesome God doesn't waste a thing. In the words of 2 Corinthians 5:17, we're talking fresh starts and new beginnings, folks! Now, the big question: Is life fair? Well, here's my take. I'm all in on a God who sent His A-game player, Jesus, to tackle sin head-on. Evil? Oh, that's just Satan's twisted tale. God's the boss here, and He can turn even our mess-ups into something good. That's the real deal, offering truth and freedom on a silver platter. Fairness level: Epic!

ELEVEN
A PEELINE TO HAPPINESS

"Nothing's funnier to me than laughing at myself."

— PHIL MCGRAW

"If you find it hard to laugh at yourself, I would be happy to do it for you."

— GROUCHO MARX

Here we go, diving into the rollercoaster ride of life with a sprinkle of humor and a dash of vivid storytelling. Picture this: You're having one of those days when all you need is a good laugh, right? The kind of day where everything seems to be going wrong, and just when you think it can't get any worse, you run out of gas. Classic.

So, let me paint you a picture of one of my recent escapades. Battling the mental fog that comes with Parkinson's, I kicked off the day with gusto. "Nothing can stop me," I thought. I was on a mission to treat myself to some Starbucks, maybe indulge in a doughnut or a cinnamon roll, and then settle in for some writing at the studio. It was shaping up to be a top-notch day.

As I pulled out onto the road, feeling like a hero for dropping off a package for my wife at the mailbox, my spirits were soaring. But then, the unthinkable happened. The car decided to call it quits right there on the road. I tried to revive it, checked the gas gauge (half a tank, phew), and then the dreaded engine warning light blinked to life. Cue the downward spiral of my once-great day.

With traffic picking up, I flicked on my hazard lights and came up with a genius plan. *I'll just push the car to the side of the road, right?* Wrong. I was stuck too close to the mailbox to open my door. After a failed attempt at some acrobatics, I realized my Kia Sportage wasn't exactly designed for non-contortionists like me. Meanwhile, cars zipped by without a care in the world.

As the plot thickened, anxiety crept in, and my tremors decided to throw a wild party, escalating to the point of no return. Instead of alarming Melinda with my car woes, I dialed up one of my sons-in-law who lived nearby. Shaun answered, "Hey, Mr. J., what's up?"

I casually greeted him before diving into my predicament.

"Shaun, my car decided to take a nap on Fern Mountain Road."

Shaun, always the problem-solver, inquired, "Did you forget to fuel up?"

"Nope, the gauge insists it's half full," I replied.

Shaun promised to hop in the shower and rush to my rescue.

"Shaun, it's a bit of a brain fog situation right now (thanks, Parkinson's), but I really need a hand ASAP," I pleaded. In a flash, Shaun and my grandson Mark swooped in, sizing up the situation of me and my beleaguered vehicle awkwardly blocking the road. With a nod of understanding, Shaun used his trusty truck to tow my car back to the safety of home. Lucky for me, having two mechanic brothers paid off as I had the car whisked away to their garage in Muskogee.

Later that day, a text from my brother Paul signaled that my ride was good to go. Melinda kindly dropped me off to retrieve the car, and as I asked Paul about the repair bill, he dropped a bombshell. "Five dollars," he stated, casually. And then the kicker, "Care to guess what the issue was?"

I was stumped. "No clue." Paul then revealed that the $5 was merely for the gas needed to kickstart the engine. Cue the crimson flush of embarrassment.

"You've got to be kidding me. My gauge showed the tank was almost half full."

"Your gauge is pulling a fast one on you, brother," Paul chuckled. Ah, the joys of my world—the whimsical, unpredictable realm of Parkinson's. But hey, let's call a spade a spade. This blunder? That's on good old aging, not Parkinson's, for a change!

Embracing the art of self-deprecating humor has been my secret weapon in navigating the twists and turns of life with PD. It's a reminder that laughter has the power to illuminate even the gloomiest days, shining a light on cherished memories that warm the heart. Many of these memories stem from my colorful journey in public ministry, where the stage was set for some truly unforgettable moments. Let's peel back the layers of time and delve into the archives of my travels, shall we?

For a glorious 15-year stretch, I orchestrated a monthly extravaganza known as the Night of Praise in the bustling Oklahoma City area. Picture a sea of over 3,000 souls gathered in harmony, soaking in the melodies that had begun to spread far and wide. My music was transcending borders, reaching the far corners of the globe, and beckoning me to share it in person. The sheer joy of hearing a crowd belt out my tunes still gives me goosebumps to this day. The early days of my musical voyage were nothing short of exhilarating, with church halls bursting at the seams, standing room only becoming the norm.

Now, let's fast forward to a memorable concert at a grand church in Fort Worth that had tongues wagging. Imagine this: eager church groups vying for prime seats, the anticipation palpable. No tickets, just pure enthusiasm. As my band and I huddled in prayer backstage, a messenger rushed in with alarming news: A scuffle had broken out over coveted seats, painting a rather dramatic picture. It felt like a scene from a battlefield report. The urgent request for me to intervene came, and as I made my way to the auditorium, a curious sight greeted me. The warring factions had miraculously found common ground and peace reigned once more. A tale as old as time, a reminder that humanity's quirks transcend all boundaries. The absurdity of a scuffle erupting over seating arrangements at a worship gathering still boggles my mind yet never fails to tickle my funny bone. Oh, the sheer peculiarity of it all!

But wait! There's more! Ah, the tales of seat-saving shenanigans! In the realm of our beloved Night of Praise in the OKC area, a familiar scene unfolded. Melinda, the maestro of seat orchestration, always ensured a special spot for our family near the stage, where my piano awaited. Just like the high-octane scene in Fort Worth, a frenzy for prime seating erupted as soon as the doors swung open to the eager crowd. One evening in OKC, a group of zealous seat savers made a bold move toward our designated family enclave. Enter my daughter Hannah, a mini version of her mama with a knack for cutting to the chase. At a tender age of around 10, Hannah spotted the seat usurpers in action and didn't hold back. "What's the deal, ladies?" she quizzed.

With unwavering confidence, one of the women claimed to be my sister.

Hannah, sharp as a tack, fired back with a truth bomb. "Well, I happen to be his daughter... and he doesn't have any sisters... so..."

The ladies swiftly beat a retreat to find refuge in another part of the auditorium.

People, oh people, always managed to sprinkle a generous dose of humor into the mix! As the Night of Praise unfolded, we found ourselves immersed in worship marathons that stretched for over three soul-stirring hours. A pause for a love offering often punctuated the proceedings, ensuring the event's financial gears kept turning smoothly. But on one memorable night, the fervor of worship reached such heights that finding a moment to break the momentum proved challenging. Yet, my bladder had other plans, reaching its bursting point and demanding attention. In a moment of unfiltered honesty, I made an impromptu announcement to the gathered throng: "Folks, we need a quick break for the love offering, and uh, I really gotta go!"

Laughter rippled through the crowd as I dashed off the stage, invoking a biblical moment with a cheeky twist. "Let the sea part!" I declared, and lo and behold, the sea of 3,000 souls parted before me as I made a mad dash (or should I say a "peeline"?) for the men's room. Sometimes, the truth, and a full bladder, truly does set you free!

Such is a day filled with unexpected twists, failed escape plans, and a touch of comedy. Life keeps us on our toes, doesn't it?

TWELVE
TRUTH VS. REALITY, PT. 2

"While we try to teach our children all about life, our children teach us what life is all about."

— ANGELA SCHWINDT

Dealing with the diagnosis of Parkinson's hasn't always been easy for me. Early on, there were times when it seemed to control my actions and attitudes, which wasn't what I wanted. Now, after living with it for over five years, I've settled into a routine shaped by not just Parkinson's, but also by the whole Covid incident (or whatever that was, lol!), my mistaken assumptions about how my kids saw me now that I felt more fragile, and my tendency to withdraw a bit from life to protect myself from getting hurt.

But here's the thing: Withdrawing from life, even temporarily, takes love off the table. To truly connect with my family, I had to step out of my own fears and risk rejection. Love, after all, demands risk. Jesus risked it all for me, knowing I might turn away...but He believed I was worth it.

When I decided to write this second volume about my life with Parkinson's, I took a big leap by asking important people in my life to share how my battle had impacted them. It was nerve-wracking, and, trust me, I've taken some big risks before, lol! I asked my children to be brutally honest about how Parkinson's has affected our family.

Reading my daughter, Glory's, response was a reality check, to say the least, and boy did I need it! But it turned out to be incredibly liberating. Her words made me feel truly seen, heard, and loved in a way that brought unexpected healing to my soul. This letter is what I like to call Glory's Reality Check:

Here are some of my thoughts on Parkinson's. My first initial reaction is that it hasn't changed much. I still view you the same. You are still the same quick-witted Dad that I know who loves to crack a joke. From my perspective, I think the primary thing that has changed is your confidence. I hate seeing you be self-conscious over the tremors. No one cares if your hand shakes. It distracts you more than other people in all reality.

It makes me sad when you apologize for moments of forgetfulness or a foggy mind. News flash: We ALL have that. You just get to blame yours on a disease. Yikes. That sounds bad even to me now that I write it. It may seem like I am being harsh. I probably am. I have a lot of feelings about it, but they may not be acceptable or understood by everyone.

Dad, you have never been one to let things get you down. You are an overcomer. I think you even wrote a song or two about that (that's a joke!). I think this diagnosis has made you

PARKINSON'S & RECREATION 2

forget that. That's ironic, isn't it? You still have all your fun knowledge and weird facts that you love to pull out of nowhere. You can recall bits of history probably better than anyone that I know. I know the brain fog is real and it wears you out. I get it. I see it, but I also know that hasn't changed who you are. It is easy for me to say this as I know I can't be in your head. I see how it wears you out sometimes when something might seem just out of reach or on the tip of your tongue. I would also like to add that this doesn't happen very often. I just want to highlight it because I see it and want others to be aware if they have a loved one who struggles with similar issues.

That leads me to another thought. I do like the representation of Sepeleo Parkinson in your Bairns of Bren book, The Puzzle. *Reading that book to the kids helped me understand how you view Parkinson's. The mind claw and the "spell" it puts you in is an interesting way of thinking about it. Looking in from the outside, I don't often think about you feeling trapped in this diagnosis. Do you feel stuck? The world passing you by and you can't respond? This brings me back to the fact that for the most part I DON'T feel like things have changed. Obviously, you could often be dealing with mental struggles and fog, and we would not notice it.*

I struggle with trying to respect you as a person and my dad, but also not wanting to baby you or pity you. You don't need my pity, but am I being too harsh? You don't need help with everything, but should I be more willing to help without you asking? You are capable, but could I step up more to lessen your burden? When do I make the transition of trying to "parent" you? I don't think I am there yet. I don't think I need to be. This leads me to my next thought.

I think this has affected Mom more than it has you, perhaps. I am just sharing my thoughts. They may not be accurate. I feel like mom tends to "baby" you or feel like she has to parent you. I think this could be a combination of you both being empty nesters and her having been in the "mom" role for so long. I think Covid made you both slow down and sequester too much. Now you don't get out as much. So then I worry that if you don't keep moving then you could slow down and really lose it. I think I am in an odd position because I hear information from you and mom and it often clashes. Maybe you are both not being honest with me. Maybe you are not being honest with yourselves or each other. Maybe you don't want to accept the truth or place blame where it doesn't belong.

I think I have been most frustrated at Mom through this. Maybe this isn't what you wanted me to write about or share. I think she feels like she has lost something and hasn't fully come to terms that this could be difficult. I think she needs to talk with someone maybe professionally and not look at Facebook Parkinson's groups, LOL!

Maybe the future she expected isn't coming true and it has made her sad. She feels like she needs something to do, so she babys you. She says she "lets" you go out and get coffee, run errands, get food, etc. I obviously do not see every waking moment, but I think it has been difficult for her. She often uses you as an excuse not to do something. She needs to get out more and doesn't feel like she can. She loves dressing up and going out but doesn't do that anymore. That's partly why I enjoyed going to the candlelight concert the other night with her. She had fun! We had fun! It was a win-win!

This may not have been what you were expecting, but you asked, so...

PARKINSON'S & RECREATION 2

Here is a fun story as well. One evening during our dinner conversation, the kids and I were talking about cheese. I think we were eating breakfast burritos and the cheese melted inside them beautifully. Mark commented that he doesn't like cheese as much, and Annabell and I agreed cheese is delicious. I told him that when I was growing up, I thought you were crazy because you didn't like cheese on food. Mark gave me the most incredulous look! I don't think he could believe that I thought you were crazy or that I could possibly say that about my DAD. Grandpa does no wrong in their eyes! Haha! Also, just note that cheese is in fact delicious and I will always eat it.

That's some raw honesty right there, and I gotta say, it resonates deep within me. I am an overcomer. My family is the reason I take on Parkinson's head-on. They're worth every battle, every risk. Glory's words hit me like a reset button for my brain, like I've been rebooted to my core beliefs. I feel like a new creation in Christ. Parkinson's isn't my defining factor. Self-pity doesn't define me. Neither do circumstances, others' opinions, or even my dislike for cheese, lol! The only definition that matters is from my Father God. Hearing my kids' perspectives makes me feel not just alive but thriving. Life gives back what you invest in it. And hey, I'll pass on the cheese. High five to Mark!

THIRTEEN
STEINWAYS AND DUCT TAPE

"I am not a famous person at home—I'm just a guy here. I'm a father, I'm a companion, I'm a human being. I am not a public figure in my house; I am not a celebrity. I am not a famous person to myself—I am just a guy."

— WILLIAM HURT

In the grand scheme of things, I'm not exactly a household name...well, maybe infamous to some! I've journeyed across the U.S. and beyond, serenading crowds with music that springs from my deep love and gratitude for God, falling under the category of Christian worship songs. You'd be surprised how many folks in evangelical circles have belted out my songs without realizing they were penned by yours truly.

Besides gracing worship concerts in churches and conferences nationwide with my music, I've often been called upon to share my personal narrative of turning away from a homosexual orientation to embrace a heterosexual lifestyle with God's guidance. I view same-sex attraction as a temptation, not a label. And that's why the infamous tag might stick better than famous in my case!

Now, this book isn't about stirring up controversies; it's about weaving my story into the fabric of Parkinson's. If you want the nitty-gritty details of my transformative journey, dive into my autobiography, *Sing Over Me*.

As I pen these words, I've just battled through a rough spell with Covid. On Father's Day, June 18, 2023, I got hit with a positive test, and my Parkinson's-ridden body took a beating. I was in agony for days, and the mental haze was almost unbearable at times. My doctor warned me that, thanks to Parkinson's, it might take anywhere from six months to two years to bounce back from the virus. Talk about a bummer. Oh, and to top it off, I completely lost my voice.

Instead of dwelling on what's gone, I'm choosing to bask in the glow of what remains—a trove of cherished memories from my days in the public eye. When I started crafting music and discovered a way to capture it, folks seemed ravenous for my tunes. All I did was pour my heart out to Father God in song, expressing my deep feelings for His love toward me.

My maiden recording venture as a worship leader/songwriter was a humble $400 production on a Tascam recorder, laying down tracks on a regular cassette tape. In its debut year, we managed to move around 60,000 cassettes (hey, youngsters, ask your grandparents about those relics, lol!). This success caught the attention of several Christian music bigwigs, waving recording contracts my way. I made it clear to each label that I couldn't sign anything that would keep me away from home for extended stretches. They raised eyebrows, insisting, "You can't sell records without hitting the road!"

My stance? "My commitment to God means safeguarding my marriage and kids above all else. Family comes first. If you can assure me that, put it in writing, and I'm in."

All three major labels I was in talks with walked away...except for one, which returned a year later in 1993 with a contract echoing my values. Since I wasn't the touring type, Word Music essentially said, "We believe in you, your music, and your story, but without tours, marketing will be minimal...scratch that, nonexistent!" I was essentially an indie artist, with Word Music acting as my distributor. Melinda and I were at peace, trusting that word of mouth would be our best bet...and guess what? God did indeed spread the music far and wide.

Between 1985 and 1993, I wore the hat of a worship pastor at a tiny inner-city church in Oklahoma City. Throughout that era and beyond, I churned out a song (or more) daily. As our melodies hit the airwaves, invites started rolling in from churches and conferences, beckoning me to share my musical creations. One memory from those days is etched in my mind forever.

A friend tagged along as we rolled up to a colossal church in Dallas for a worship event. The parking lot chaos felt like a scene from a Black Friday sale, with folks jostling for spots like it was a brawl over a big screen TV! I was utterly bewildered, clueless about the frenzy unfolding before me. I blurted out, "What's with this crowd?!"

My buddy shot me a look of disbelief mixed with a hint of horror and quipped, "They're here for YOU, you goofball!" Well, the actual word used was a bit harsher, but let's keep it light.

I retorted, "You must be kidding me!" Yet, as it turned out, the turnout that night was so massive that we had to cram people into every nook and cranny, from the choir loft to the stage, sprawling around me and the piano, with attendees spilling into aisles, perching on the floor and leaning against walls. We pushed the fire code to its limit and then some. Back in those early days of my public journey, such scenes were not uncommon. Folks were yearning for connection, grappling with deep-seated emotional wounds, and buckling under the weight of hidden fears and failures. I believe they flocked to my concerts because they found a safe space to be real, to unburden themselves. They resonated with my candid confessions to God through music and storytelling.

In those unforgettable moments of worship, it wasn't unusual to witness a sea of tears flowing freely. I often called out individuals with specific needs, inviting them to rise so I could serenade them with the heart of God. On one poignant occasion, I invited those grappling with suicidal thoughts to stand. Within seconds, a wave of souls rose across the vast auditorium, with estimates suggesting over 50 hearts bared their struggles. As I sang God's love over them, fellow believers encircled them, offering prayers. Before I knew it, all 2,500 souls present that night were swept up in a cathartic release, weeping as they embraced the first step towards healing: raw honesty.

PARKINSON'S & RECREATION 2

I could feel the fervor in the air as folks poured out their hearts to God, celebrating newfound intimacy and triumph in His presence. The worship crescendos would often escalate into jubilant outbursts, with worshippers twirling in unbridled joy. The zeal would reach such heights that warnings had to be issued to the balcony attendees at venues in Del City, Okla., and Waco, Texas, to temper their movements to prevent potential structural mishaps!

Sometimes, the energy of the crowd and the thunderous worship compelled me to pound the piano keys with such abandon that the keyboard cover repeatedly clattered down onto my hands. At one juncture, the cover's incessant descent forced me to enlist a helper to prop it up or find a solution. In true Southern church fashion, the next thing I knew, the piano's majestic nine-foot Steinway lid was held open with a trusty strip of duct tape. It was a sight that elicited a mix of amusement and discomfort—a chuckle at the sight of a duct-taped Steinway and a cringe at the thought of adhesive tarnishing the instrument's grandeur.

In the whirlwind of my concert and public ministry days, I always preferred a genuine piano, though that wish wasn't always granted. I can't even begin to tally the number of keyboards that couldn't withstand my relentless key pounding, resulting in the instrument tumbling into my lap, requiring a pair of men to flank me and hold it steady as I carried on tickling the ivories!

As I reflect on those vibrant years, a flood of memories cascades through my mind, each deserving its own chapter. Like the instance when I cued my drummer, only to pivot and witness him toppling backward from his throne, crashing to the ground with a resounding thud. I had to halt the concert to explain the mishap to the audience. My heart went out to him, replaying the moment I metaphorically reached out, only to witness him descending in slow motion into the orchestra pit's shadows. These vivid snapshots are etched into my memory, serving as reminders that even in the battle against Parkinson's, each triumph, no matter how modest, is a victory worth celebrating.

FOURTEEN
ANNABELL & MARK

"You get what you get and don't throw a fit."

— ANNABELL THOMPSON, AGE 6

Writing this second book about my life with Parkinson's holds deep meaning for me, as it serves as a testament of faith and hope for the generations that will follow in our ever-expanding family lineage. With our family tree growing rapidly, I feel compelled to document at least my and Melinda's chapter in this flourishing legacy.

Speaking of family dynamics, a recent anecdote involving our granddaughter, Annabell, and her mother, our daughter Glory, perfectly encapsulates the delightful quirkiness that runs in our family. Annabell and her clever brother, Mark, possess sharp wits and infectious humor, serving as a limitless source of heartwarming amusement and soul-soothing moments.

Glory graciously shared some priceless Annabell anecdotes from our family chat, and I can't help but share them verbatim for their sheer charm:

"I was explaining Pei Wei and P.F. Chang's to the kids. Told them how we used to go with friends, and dad and I would go on dates there.
Annabell asks, 'You have friends?'"

"Annabell was reading us a book last night and got tickled and Mark and I were annoyed but then couldn't help but giggle. She has an infectious laugh."

"Annabell wanted to wear her pjs but I told her no, since she has to go with me to my office while I'm on the floor (Glory is a realtor). She said, 'I guess I can't look beautiful.' And walked away." (Classic Annabell)

Annabell, watching cartoons:
No one: (silence)
Annabell: "I feel like I want to bite someone."
Glory: "Oh yeah?"
Annabell: "Yeah, I haven't bit someone in a long time."
Chomps teeth

On another note, Annabell's dream of owning an ice cream truck and featuring The Knuckle Song as its jingle showcases her endearing confidence and musical prowess. This piano duet, predominantly played on black keys with knuckles, has become a favorite among our grandchildren, with Annabell proudly claiming to be self-taught. Her spirit is truly a treasure!

Glory shared the story that occurred during a cozy evening. "Annabell took the reins as the storyteller, navigating through a book until she stumbled upon the word 'though.' In a bid to assist, I gently reminded her, 'Remember how t-h makes a *th* sound like in *the*?" To my surprise and slight amusement, she promptly retorted, 'Well, it doesn't in Thompson.'"
Oh, the quirks of the English language!

A delightful summer surprise unfolded when Brad Henderson, a dear friend and talented musician, along with Ryan Dahl from PraiseCharts.com, graced us with their presence in 2023. Our home buzzed with the chatter of kids and grandkids eager to meet them. Little Annabell, with her precocious nature, engaged Brad in a conversation about her ice cream truck dreams. Brad, ever enthusiastic, shared a peanut butter ice cream recipe with her, painting a vivid picture of melting peanut butter to create a delectable shell over the ice cream.
Annabell's deadpan response after the elaborate explanation? "But I'm allergic to peanuts." Classic Annabell, stealing the show with her candid charm!

From my earliest days I've had a penchant for collecting items that hold sentimental value to me. Whether it's old hymnals, antique bottles from the 1800s, musical instruments, or even prized signed baseballs like the one autographed by Nolan Ryan, each piece tells a story close to my heart. During a conversation with my grandson Mark, as I shared the stories behind my eclectic collections, his innocent curiosity led to a candid question that caught me off guard.

In a moment of raw vulnerability, Mark mustered the courage to ask, "Grandpa, can I have this when you die?" The weight of his words hung heavy in the air, his eyes welling up with tears as he grappled with the reality of mortality. Embracing him tenderly, I reassured Mark that it's okay to discuss such matters with me, emphasizing the inevitability of death and the promise of eternal life through faith in Jesus Christ. Our heartfelt exchange brought solace to his young heart, easing his fears and sparking a profound conversation about life's transient nature and the hope of reunion in the afterlife.

Encouraging Mark to explore my stuff and compile a wish list of items he treasures, I initiated a lighthearted family tradition that has since evolved into a playful joke. Now, if anyone in the family desires a keepsake from my collection, they humorously stake their claim by discreetly tagging it with a piece of paper bearing their name! I can't help but beam with pride over Mark for myriad reasons, and one recent instance that truly showcased his leadership skills was during the student council campaign speeches. Picture this: Mark, armed with his unwavering determination and using voice-to-text technology, crafted a compelling address all on his own.

Let me give you a sneak peek at part one of his speech:

"Hi, my name is Mark, and I am in fourth grade. I would like you to vote for me because I am a great student and have

great grades. My first idea is to stop bullying and ensure everyone is treated equally, including teachers. If you vote for me, I believe we can bring more freedom and fun parties to our school."

His eloquence and vision left me in awe, drawing parallels to my own youthful aspirations as a student council candidate, 4-H president, and FFA president. But what truly warms my heart is our shared love for basketball—a bond that transcends generations and echoes through time. As fate would have it, both in my high school days and on Mark's current team, we stood out as the sole white players, a delightful coincidence that never fails to bring a smile to my face. The juxtaposition of our team photos side by side is a visual testament to the enduring legacy of passion for the game that we both hold dear.

Labor Day weekend in 2023 brought a lively gathering of kids and grandkids to our abode, culminating in refreshing pool sessions each afternoon. However, my recent cataract surgery imposed certain restrictions, relegating me to a poolside perch due to the no-lifting and no-bending rules. Clad in oversized sunglasses perched atop my regular glasses, Annabell's astute observation added a touch of whimsy to the situation. With a single glance, she sagely remarked, "They make you look very professional." Suddenly, I felt elevated from a mere lump of playdough to a distinguished figure, courtesy of Annabell's keen eye and knack for humor!

As the sun dipped below the horizon, our evenings were marked by hearty family meals and refreshing swims. However, one Sunday evening brought a hilarious delay when Mark and Annabell arrived late. Inquiring about the tardiness, Melinda probed Annabell, who candidly revealed the culinary ordeal that caused the delay. "We had to eat peas. Mark gagged on them. We had to try everything mom cooked, and we almost couldn't come over!" A true saga of veggie aversion!

Melinda sought clarification from Glory, who confirmed the pea-induced drama, recounting how she served salmon and mashed cauliflower alongside a few sugar snap peas, much to Mark and Annabell's dismay. While the salmon was a hit, the peas sparked a revolt, with Mark reacting as if his world had crumbled, despite once adoring the green legumes straight from the plant.

In a heartfelt message to my grandchildren, I shared a quirky family trait: my lifelong aversion to peas. The taste, texture, smell, and sight of peas have always made me queasy. Recalling my childhood tactics of discreetly depositing peas into my milk to avoid them, I humorously noted that this disdain for peas is ingrained in our DNA, passing down this peculiar trait to the next generation. Peas: the ultimate nemesis, uniting generations in a shared distaste!

FIFTEEN
DADDY'S TOO SMALL

"Quote me as saying I was misquoted."

— GROUCHO MARX

Throughout my life, I've journeyed through peaks of joy and valleys of despair. In moments of darkness, I find solace in memories of divine intervention, bringing a serene calm to my soul. And in times of tranquility, I embrace the notion that even in the grip of Parkinson's, God weaves purpose into every circumstance. As the disease tightens its hold, my quest for laughter and joy grows stronger, becoming my daily mission.

Seeking mirth and delight, I often reminisce about the comical episodes from my years in public ministry, where Melinda and I raised our brood of nine children amidst the whirlwind of our work. Our kids were born within a remarkable 10-year span that left many bewildered. Concerts were a family affair, with our tribe of little ones in tow.

For a decade and a half, we hosted a Night of Praise every first Friday in Oklahoma City, a tradition our children grew up immersed in. Familiar with the ins and outs of these events, the kids had free rein to explore the vast church venue where the gatherings took place. Whether manning the merchandise table with my parents, peddling books, CDs, and even cassette tapes, or engaging in spirited games of hide and seek within the labyrinthine church, the pre- and post-concert hours were a playground for our youngsters. During music and ministry, our children found their own adventures, turning every event into a blend of work and play.

I remember one hilarious incident every time I spot a communion table at the front of a church sanctuary. After each concert, I made it a point to connect with anyone seeking a chat, resulting in lines that could stretch for an hour. These post-show gatherings attracted folks eager to express gratitude for spiritual moments or share their deepest struggles. I made sure to stay until every person had their say, believing that simply listening was a gesture of acknowledging their worth.

During one bustling meet-and-greet session, as the auditorium buzzed with departing concertgoers and my kids either assisted with sales or played quietly in the background, chaos ensued. Amidst the joyful hum of chatter, my wife's voice pierced through the noise, commanding our children to vacate the stage promptly. And they complied without hesitation. But it was her subsequent directive that still cracks me up to this day.

PARKINSON'S & RECREATION 2

With unyielding authority, Melinda hollered at the kids, "Stop jumping over the communion table!" In that split second, I witnessed one of my sons executing a gravity-defying leap from the stage, effortlessly soaring over the sizable table with the finesse of Spider Man, executing a flawless landing that could rival an Olympic gymnast. The scene replayed in my mind like a cinematic masterpiece in slow motion. Sure, I was initially taken aback by the perceived disrespect (as per the church code), but deep down, I couldn't help a twinge of pride for my son's impeccable technique, impressive height, flawless distance, and that picture-perfect landing. Way to go, son!

Recalling my travel adventures always unearths a trove of delightful tales. Take, for instance, the years I spent touring with a band, often in the company of my manager at the time, Kathy Law. On a memorable trip to Mississippi, our journey began with a flight into New Orleans, where the sponsoring church's pastor awaited to chauffeur us.

Since our flight schedule had left us famished, the pastor kindly suggested we dine at one of his go-to restaurants. The anticipation of the trip and the prospect of a hearty meal had me buzzing with giddy excitement. When we were seated at our table, Kathy excused herself for a brief restroom break.

As the savory scents of Cajun cuisine enveloped us, our server arrived with menus in hand. Amid the tantalizing array of dishes, the pastor recommended an appetizer he held dear, proclaiming, "I highly recommend the broccoli balls. They're my favorite."

Seizing the comedic moment, I quipped, "I didn't even know broccoli HAD balls!" This prompted a chorus of chuckles from the band, akin to mischievous adolescents, until an uncomfortable hush fell over us in response to the pastor's silence. Awkward, yet undeniably hilarious!

While we quietly returned to our menus, Kathy rejoined the table. As she perused her menu, the pastor reiterated his endorsement of the infamous broccoli balls. Unfazed, Kathy delivered her punchline with precision, echoing my sentiment, "I didn't even know broccoli HAD balls!"

Once again, our attempts to stifle laughter were futile, with Kathy's timely quip leaving the pastor visibly flustered. Sensing the awkward tension, Kathy swiftly shifted focus back to the meal, declaring, "I don't think we need any appetizers. I'm starving. Let's dig in." The lingering awkwardness morphed into an even funnier moment, embodying the essence of a 65-year-old man-boy reveling in the humor. You're welcome.

During my years of hosting worship conferences, I decided to spice things up once by introducing a songwriting contest into the event lineup. The two criteria were that the songs had to be original and centered on the Lord. Each submission required a music lead sheet, the story behind the song, and a recording of the piece. Little did I anticipate the overwhelming response this contest would elicit.

PARKINSON'S & RECREATION 2

As soon as I unveiled the contest, a flood of entries poured in, totaling around 100 submissions. While most entries arrived on CDs, a few stragglers clung to the antiquated charm of cassette tapes. Despite the inferior sonic quality of the tapes, I embarked on the Herculean task of listening to each entry, determined to unearth the cream of the crop. After much deliberation, I identified the top three entries, earmarked for special recognition with a gift, a modest cash prize, and the coveted promotion to my extensive email list.

As I immersed myself in the plethora of submissions, one song struck a chord of familiarity beyond its melody. It wasn't just the tune that resonated with me but the voices behind it—or should I say, the trio of voices. Upon scrutinizing the entrant's name, "Doris and the Daisies," and the song title, "The Fire Song," it dawned on me that this melody had a nostalgic ring to it. A trip down memory lane unveiled that this song had echoed through my childhood, serenaded to me by none other than my mischievously witty mother. Dating back to 1929, the song had etched itself into my memory. And as for the vocalists on the recording, well, let's just say I knew them all too well. My mother, the prankster extraordinaire, had conspired with her equally humorous sisters, my aunts Patsy and Annie, to record the song, attempting to pull a fast one on me. Alas, their comedic endeavor fell short in my discerning ear.

If you're familiar with my tales, you'll know of my adoration for Doris Day and her iconic tune, "Que Sera, Sera," and how in my nightly reveries, Doris Day assumed the role of my mother, with my father portrayed as none other than Captain James Tiberius Kirk. Indulge me for a moment here. The trio's moniker alone should have raised a red flag, but it wasn't until I immersed myself in their song that the penny dropped on the identities of these crafty songsters. And so, my scheme began to unfold.

As the much-anticipated conference unfolded and the time arrived to unveil the top three contenders and crown the victor, I teased the audience with the promise of a special consolation prize for a truly unique entrant. With a mischievous glint in my eye, I instructed the sound technician to cue up the mystery song. The initial notes reverberated through the air, prompting uproarious laughter from my father, audible all the way from the book table in the church foyer. Meanwhile, my mother attempted to shield her face with both hands, well aware of the impending comedic reveal.

As the curious tune, reminiscent of something Lucy and Ethel might have belted out, drew to a close—originally penned by the renowned hymnist B.B. McKinney—I regaled the audience with the intriguing backstory behind this eccentric entry and unveiled the true identities of Doris and the Daisies. Inviting my mother, Peggy a.k.a. Doris, to join me on stage, I presented her with a framed certificate commemorating her near-miss in pulling off yet another of her and her sisters' legendary pranks. Two moments stood out vividly for me during this episode: the infectious sound of my father's laughter echoing from the foyer and the gleeful satisfaction of watching my mother accept her tongue-in-cheek award, secure in the knowledge that I had seen through her and her sisters'

PARKINSON'S & RECREATION 2

antics all along. My sole lament? That her partners-in-crime, my aunts, were absent from this delightful caper.

Throughout the years, our worship conferences have been a treasure trove of unforgettable moments. Once, my savvy manager, Kathy, took the reins of doling out door prizes to the eager attendees. The first prize hinged on a simple question: How many children did Melinda and I have? The subsequent prize required participants to name at least five of my offspring—a tad on the stalker-ish side, in hindsight. And the stakes rose for the third prize, where contenders had to recall at least three of my music recordings. Amidst the buzz of anticipation, a zealous woman thrust herself into the spotlight, clamoring, "Me! Me!"

Kathy obliged.

With two correct titles swiftly identified, the suspense mounted as the lady struggled to pinpoint the third album. Now, picture this: I have a track named "Daddy's Song" and another titled "No Life Too Small." After a brief mental hiccup, she triumphantly declared, "I've got it!" The room held its breath, bracing for her revelation, and boy did she deliver! Bursting with certainty, she proclaimed, "Daddy's too small!"

The moment those words escaped her lips, I involuntarily spewed water all over the piano where I was perched, ready for the next session. Kathy shot me a look of disbelief and exclaimed, "She said, 'Daddy's Too Small'!"—prompting an uproar of laughter that reverberated through the room. I found myself collapsing onto the floor, consumed by uncontrollable, rib-tickling belly laughs, as Kathy and I repeatedly succumbed to fits of mirth at each other's expense. It was a moment of pure joy and hilarity that has since etched itself as one of the fondest memories of my life.

SIXTEEN
DOSES OF JOY: GRAHAM CRAPPERS AND GROOT FRUIT

Author and lecturer Leo Buscaglia once talked about a contest he was asked to judge. The purpose of the contest was to find the most caring child. The winner was a 4-year-old child whose next-door neighbor was an elderly gentleman who had recently lost his wife. Upon seeing the man cry, the little boy went into the old gentleman's yard, climbed onto his lap, and just sat there. When his mother asked what he had said to the neighbor, the little boy said, "Nothing, I just helped him cry."

That story perfectly encapsulates the immeasurable worth of my grandchildren. Now, you might be thinking, *Geez, this Jernigan guy really goes on about his grandkids!* And hey, I get it. But there's a simple reason behind it. They bring me immense joy amid life's challenges, playing a crucial role in alleviating my struggles. Grandchildren have this magical ability to make us feel cherished, indispensable, and loved—even when we might feel like a bit of a burden at times. Their mere presence has this incredible power to uplift my spirits without them even saying a word. It's like being wrapped in a warm blanket of love. And speaking of love, let me share a quote I recently stumbled upon that beautifully captures what my words can't quite express:

> "When someone loves you, the way they say your name is different. You just know that your name is safe in their mouth."
>
> — BILLY, AGE 4

Isn't that just heartwarming? That feeling is exactly what I experience when I hear one of my grandchildren call out, "Grandpa!"—it's pure love and reverence in those simple words. Now, let me give you a glimpse of how my grandkids help slow down the progression of Parkinson's disease in my life.

I've got this shirt that boldly proclaims, "Grandpa. The man. The myth. The legend."

When my granddaughter, Mia, saw it, she nodded and said, "That shirt is so true." Talk about a confidence boost!

Then there was the time when our granddaughter, Abigail, decided to have her 7th birthday bash at a trampoline park. My response to the invite? "Imagine the epic footage of a Parkinson's grandpa on a trampoline—'Terrific Trademark Trampoline Tremors!'" Sadly, I didn't make it to the party, so no such video exists...yet a grandpa can dream, right?

PARKINSON'S & RECREATION 2

Recently, I joined my son-in-law, Chip, on a fishing trip with his two boys. Theo, the elder one, reeled in two decent-sized bass all by himself, while the younger Edison proudly caught four on his own. My role? Well, I became the official weed remover from hooks, the rescuer of lures stuck in tree branches, and the untangler of Theo and Edison's crossed fishing lines (which happened quite frequently!). In a hilarious mishap, their lines got so tangled that they even managed to loop one around my ear —a sight that sent them into fits of laughter!

Instead of helping me sort out the mess, they decided to playfully wrap me up in even more line. Their infectious giggles soon had me in stitches, escalating into uncontrollable laughter! Eventually, I had to send them back to their dad to unravel the fishing line chaos. Oh, how I wish I had captured that moment on video—it was pure comedy gold!

Theo, at the sprightly age of 4 as of this writing, is a bundle of energy with a sharp wit and an impressive vocabulary. He's a treasure trove of quotes and humor. Sometimes, he'll grab a book, settle into my lap, and "read" it to me in his version of Spanish, which sounds like gibberish but with such conviction that I start to wonder if he's onto something!

During a game of Hide-and-Seek, I swiftly discovered him crouching behind a chair nearby. "Found ya!" I exclaimed.

Quick as a flash, he retorted, "You can't see us if you can't hear us. If you can't hear us, you can't find us."

Perplexed, I replied, "That makes no sense!" This simple exchange sent him into a fit of giggles, and we both shared a moment of pure joy and laughter that warmed my heart.

Here we go with more delightful Theo quotes! Picture this: Theo refers to graham crackers as "The graham crappers!"—a classic mix-up that never fails to draw a chuckle.

Another Theo gem: "Mom, I need ibuprofen for my hiccups because they keep waking me up." Pure genius, that Theo!

During a livestream worship service at church, Theo spotted an older man drumming and expresses his concern, exclaiming, "An old guy is playing drums!? That's not good! He could die while he's playing drums!" Oh, the innocence and wisdom of children!

Meanwhile, Theo's little brother, Edison, requests a "piggy ride back" instead of a "piggyback ride."

And here's a cute one: Our daughter, Galen, assumes the role of a witch with Turkish delight in a magical game of Narnia with Edison and Theo. As she ventures into the enchanted playroom, young Theo shouts, "Hey, witch! Wait up!"

Edison's adorable mispronunciation of "Groot" as "fruit" is absolutely precious. At just 2 years old, his innocent charm shines through. And when he found out I was sick with Covid, his heartfelt words melted my heart: "I don't want Grandpa to ever, ever be sick!"

From a humorous moment in our Family WhatsApp Chat, Raina shares how watching football led Edison to dub the San Diego Chargers "The Unpluggers" after a game against the Dallas Cowboys. Kids really do have the best interpretations!

And let's not forget about Zella, our lively 5-year-old granddaughter, who never fails to bring a smile to my face. According to her mom, during a car ride home, Zella suddenly declared, "Mama, I just figured something out! Crashing into houses is illegal!" Sometimes, the simplest observations are the most profound!

Zella's mischievous side also shines through as she loves to play pranks on me and Melinda. Despite our best efforts, she manages to sneak up on us with ninja-like stealth. It's become a fun challenge trying to outsmart her, but I'm convinced she's secretly part ninja herself!

On a sunny afternoon, the delightful Zella burst into our bedroom, eager to give Melinda a hug. With the innocence only a 5-year-old possesses, Zella exclaimed, "Grandma! You have boobies! My mom has boobies, too! And my mommy's boobies are bigger than yours!" And just like that, she confidently sauntered out of the room, leaving us in fits of laughter. Oh, the candid observations of children—truly a balm for the soul!

In another hilarious encounter shared by Annē, Zella showcased her dramatic flair at the farmer's market. Eyeing some cookies at a booth, she spotted the price tag, let out an exasperated, "Oh, man! I like free cookies," and stomped away in a burst of theatricality. Pure Zella gold!

These moments are precious doses of joy that remind me of life's true treasures. These seemingly insignificant interactions hold immense value in my heart, never to fade away like morning mist on a pond. They are etched into my memories, enriching my existence with profound meaning and depth. To put it frankly, these moments are my life—they encapsulate the essence of what truly matters.

SEVENTEEN
WHAT CAUSED MY PARKINSON'S

Just what is Parkinson's Disease? According to Parkinson.org/NewlyDiagnosed:

Parkinson's is a progressive neurological disorder that causes a gradual loss of brain cells that produce dopamine. In the U.S., nearly one million people live with PD and about 90,000 people are diagnosed each year. Parkinson's (PD) is typically diagnosed after 60, but people under 50 can also have young-onset PD (YOPD).

What are early signs of Parkinson's?
- *Tremor*
- *Small Handwriting*
- *Loss of Smell*
- *Trouble Sleeping*
- *Trouble Moving or Walking*
- *Constipation*
- *Soft or Low Voice*
- *Masked Face (less expressive)*
- *Dizziness or Fainting*

- *Stooping or Hunching Over*

Do Parkinson's symptoms change over time?
Every person's experience with PD is unique, as is the rate of its progression. Symptoms progress over time and can be both movement-related or non-movement related. Many people with PD experience depression, anxiety and/or apathy. We encourage you to talk to your doctor about any symptoms that interfere with everyday life.

What causes Parkinson's?
The honest answer is there is no known specific cause of Parkinson's. There is some evidence that 10% to 15% of those with PD have similar genetic markers...but even in those cases there is nothing definitive. Genetics cause about 10 to 15% of all PD. In the other 85 to 90% of cases, the specific cause is unknown.

There is a growing body of evidence suggesting that environmental factors may play a role in the development of Parkinson's. These factors include head injuries, geographic location, and exposure to pesticides, among others.

While some attribute PD to a mix of genetics, environment, and lifestyle, my family history offers no record of PD, leading me to question the genetic influence in my case.

Reflecting on my past, I recall the heavy use of pesticides and insecticides on our farm during my early days. Additionally, relocating to my childhood farm in 1993 and subsequently settling in our current farm for the past 25 years exposed me to various environmental factors.

PARKINSON'S & RECREATION 2

Although I have occasionally used herbicides for weed control, always taking precautions like wearing a mask, I find it hard to believe that these factors have significantly impacted my PD diagnosis.

The factors I believe have played a more substantial role in my journey with Parkinson's are the physical, emotional, and mental pressures I have faced throughout my life. Sharing my experiences of deliverance from SSA, facing opposition and threats, enduring the pain of those with differing views trying to invalidate my life's work, and losing friendships over spiritual disagreements have caused immense emotional burdens and mental strain. The sense of isolation and abandonment, especially within the church community, following instances of being "canceled," has been particularly challenging and isolating. Dealing with these pressures has been far from easy, to say the least. No walk in the Parkinson's…

As Melinda and I delved deeper into the environmental factors potentially linked to my PD, we couldn't ignore the impact of multiple surgeries and the repercussions of anesthesia on my body and mind. From hernia repairs to shoulder and knee surgeries, it struck me as somewhat ironic that my pursuit of a healthy lifestyle led me down the path of these medical interventions!

Being active and sports-driven has been a cornerstone of my life. Basketball has always held a special place in my heart, a passion I continue to share with my grandchildren to this day. Tennis also became a significant part of my routine, with biweekly matches spanning countless years. And let's not forget my daily three-mile runs over two decades—apparently, the very activities meant to keep me healthy ended up taking a toll on my shoulders and knees—the ultimate irony!

Following my initial rotator cuff surgery, a peculiar pattern emerged. Moments of overwhelming feelings crept in, initially unrecognized but later identified as panic attacks. Sleep became elusive, and the idea of taking pain medication seemed to exacerbate the sense of losing control over my mind. Eventually, I realized that it was the pain, not the medication, triggering these panic episodes.

During this challenging period, I honed a proactive approach to combat impending panic attacks. The strategy was simple yet profound. At the first inkling of an attack, I turned to my incredible wife, Melinda, seeking her grounding presence. Without hesitation, she would shower me with words of truth, listing all the blessings and positives in my life, a beacon of light amid inner turmoil.

Melinda's words of reassurance became my anchor during turbulent times. "You have nine amazing children. You have grandchildren who absolutely adore you. You have a wife who loves you and stands steadfastly by your side. You have a vast audience touched by your music and ministry. You have friends who have been unwavering in your darkest hours. You have the loving presence of the Lord Jesus with you always. You are not alone. You are an overcomer. You win no matter what." These declarations, rooted in God's truth and boundless love, had a profound calming effect on my soul, extinguishing fear with each utterance.

PARKINSON'S & RECREATION 2

The transformative power of love was evident as fear dissipated in the presence of such affirmations. My wife orchestrated a heartfelt gesture involving our children that remains a cherished memory. Each child penned uplifting scriptures, words of admiration, or even cheeky dad jokes on small paper strips. Melinda presented me with a jar filled with these notes, instructing me to reach for one whenever a panic attack loomed. This jar of heartfelt sentiments stands as one of the most precious gifts I have ever received. Over the years, they have replenished this jar of hope, encouragement, joy, and love, a tangible reservoir of strength in times of need.

Melinda and I observed a lingering impact of anesthesia on my mind post-surgery, surpassing the physical recovery timeline. I am convinced that anesthesia has left a lasting imprint on my neurological system, playing a significant role in the emergence of panic attacks and ultimately contributing to the development of Parkinson's Disease in my life.

Reflecting on significant events, I've come to recognize another profound influence on the development of Parkinson's disease in my life—the heart-wrenching process of witnessing my father's decline over the span of several weeks. In the summer of 2017, my father's health began to deteriorate, marked by a series of debilitating falls. The tipping point arrived when my mother, unable to assist him after a fall and alarmed by his incoherent speech, summoned an ambulance. I vividly recall the rush, driving 16 miles from my home to my parents' residence just in time to witness him being carefully loaded onto the stretcher and into the ambulance. Trailing the ambulance to the hospital, a cocktail of fear, dread, and sorrow enveloped me during that solemn journey.

For those agonizing 20 minutes behind the ambulance, my thoughts were a jumble of prayers for my father and mother, whispered truths to soothe my own soul, and tears that flowed freely. In the ensuing weeks, as my father's health fluctuated within hospital walls, the stark reality of his impending departure weighed heavily on my brothers, my mother, and myself. I can still recall the nights spent at his bedside, giving my mother respite, only to be met with the gut-wrenching sounds of his pain-filled moans. These moments stirred echoes of my own battles with fear and panic attacks.

Facing the rawness of mortality, what pierced me to the core was hearing my father's desperate cries, his voice tinged with longing and anguish as he called out, "Daddy, I need you! Daddy, where are you? Daddy! Daddy! Daddy!" In that poignant instant, instinct guided me to grasp his hand, offering solace in the reassurance that he was not alone.

Each plea for his father was met with my steady response, "It's going to be alright. I'm here. You are not alone."

In the tender final moments with my father, my three brothers and I, a quartet of boys, took turns keeping vigil at his bedside. Amidst the haze of delirium that often shrouded him, there were precious intervals of clarity. It was during these lucid spells that we orchestrated poignant farewells, summoning our children and his grandchildren to pay their last respects.

PARKINSON'S & RECREATION 2

One such moment stands out vividly when our daughter Hannah, calling from across the seas in Australia via FaceTime, implored her grandfather, "Grandpa, can you hold on for two more weeks? I'm bringing my family over, and I want your great-granddaughters to meet you. Can you hold on for me?"

My father, mustering his strength, replied, "I will hold on for you."

In the ensuing weeks, we cocooned ourselves in a tapestry of cherished family memories. Among the gems of those days was the poignant exchange when I assured him of his eternal remembrance through the book I was crafting—a tribute to a remarkable act of love he had bestowed upon me in my youth. This book, *The Incredible Growing Basketball Goal*, a tale woven with the threads of his sacrificial love for me, was slated for publication in October. However, driven by an urgent desire to share this legacy with my father, I implored my publisher to expedite a special preview copy. With unwavering dedication, the publisher rushed a demo of the book to me. As I turned the pages with my father, revealing the enchanting illustrations that mirrored our shared story, tears of nostalgia and tears of love cascaded down our faces.

One touching memory that lingers close to my heart unfolded in the sterile confines of the ICU, where my father lay mute beneath the mechanical hum of a ventilator that sustained his fragile breath. Frustration etched on his face as he struggled to convey a pressing need, thwarted by the barrier of speechlessness. My attempts to decipher his silent pleas—ranging from summoning the nurse to fetching a drink of water—only seemed to compound his exasperation. My mother's efforts yielded no breakthrough, and even my brothers left the room perplexed.

Then, a ray of hope emerged in the form of my son Ezra, who journeyed from Oklahoma City to Muskogee to stand by his grandfather's side. Adhering to the ICU's visitor limit, I escorted Ezra to meet his grandpa, recounting our prior struggles in understanding his unspoken desire. With a gentle touch, Ezra leaned in, locking gazes with my father, and posed the simple question, "What is it that you need, Grandpa?"

In response, a symphony of groans and subtle gestures from my father were met by Ezra's insightful deduction. "Do you need your bed raised so you can see us better?" A nod from my dad, accompanied by a sigh of relief that spoke volumes, signaled a breakthrough in communication. In that transformative instant, Ezra was christened "The Grandpa Whisperer," unraveling the enigma that had confounded us all.

True to his promise, my father clung to life until the long-awaited arrival of Hannah and her family from across the seas. On August 30, 2017, amidst a rare moment of clarity, my daughter, her husband Ash, and their little girls, Elliott and Matilda, shared a fleeting yet profound connection with my father. The beauty of that encounter was etched in my memory as a poignant testament to love and family bonds.

Tragedy struck the following morning, shrouding us in sorrow as my father departed this world around 5:30 a.m. on August 31, 2017. Grief was heavy on my soul in the ensuing weeks, prompting me to seek solace from

PARKINSON'S & RECREATION 2

one of my life's guiding lights, spiritual mentor Jack Taylor. His compassionate gesture of sending a plane ticket whisked me away to Florida for a week of healing and soul-nourishing guidance. Amidst the balm of his wisdom, the vast expanse of loss began to stir.

My mind had become a home for burdens that were never mine to bear. In a subtle shift, I found myself donning the cloak of a victim rather than embracing the mantle of a victor. It was as if my human psyche had embarked on a covert mission to reset its factory settings—a divine nudge, perhaps, urging me to pause, savor life's moments, and realign my priorities.

The relentless cadence of years of ministry, a litany of surgeries, and the relentless siege of panic attacks had etched their marks upon my soul, culminating in the unassuming tremor that first manifested in the pinky of my right hand—a subtle harbinger, a faint tremor that whispered of the impending storm. A seismic jolt that prompted a profound reevaluation of my journey. In the crucible of this diagnosis, Parkinson's emerged as a quintessential reset moment—a pivotal juncture that summoned me to navigate uncharted waters with resilience and grace.

EIGHTEEN
I DIDN'T SEE THAT COMING

"The only thing worse than being blind is having sight but no vision."

— HELEN KELLER

You might find this little quirk of mine a tad peculiar (as if you needed more evidence), but during that tumultuous phase of my life, I realized something fascinating. Each night, as I drifted into slumber, a melody serenaded my mind, only to be swiftly replaced by a different tune come morning light. This curious musical carousel, with its ever-changing soundtrack, held me captive. And so, I embarked on the whimsical experiment of documenting this nocturnal symphony in my journal. Brace yourself for a peek into the melodic musings of my subconscious!

June 14 - Drifted off to the tune of "For He's a Jolly Good Fellow"

June 15 - Awakened to the strains of Ed Sheeran's "Perfect;" lulled to sleep by "Nobody Fills My Heart Like Jesus"

June 16 - Greeted the day with the jaunty notes of "Yankee Doodle" and bid adieu to nightfall with the comforting hymns of "Amazing Grace" and "Thank You, Lord"

June 17 - A mysterious melody greeted my awakening; slumber beckoned with the iconic "Star Wars Theme"

June 18 - Tunes of "Thank You, Lord" and "This Day" marked Father's Day 2023; dreams woven with "Folsom Prison Blues"

June 19 - The jingle of a Burger King commercial roused me from sleep; embraced by the melody of "Surround Me" (during my bout with Covid)

June 20 - Stirred by "Who Can Satisfy My Soul" at dawn; lulled by the melancholic strains of "Both Sides Now" at dusk

June 21 - "Life Is a Highway" set the morning's tempo; nightfall resonated with the uplifting chorus of "Lord, I Lift Your Name On High"

June 22 - Awakened by the sacred notes of "Lord, I Lift Your Name On High;" drifted into slumber to the nostalgic croon of "Puppy Love"

June 23 - Christmas cheer in June with "We Wish You a Merry Christmas;" embraced by the modern rhythm of "Shape of You" as sleep's embrace beckoned

June 24 - A random melody kicked off the day; dreamscape painted with the anthemic "Eye of the Tiger"

June 25 - Another day, another spontaneous melody; lulled to rest by the soul-stirring "I Lay My Heart Down"

This strange symphony went on for twelve more nights! I don't know what prompted me to share my quirky little experiment with you. Perhaps shedding light on the musical journal I meticulously maintained for those fleeting weeks will offer some clarity. If it does, drop me a line and share your thoughts! There was an odd comfort in having my mind enveloped in melodies as I drifted off to sleep and as I woke—I can almost hear your silent sigh of relief, "Thank goodness for small miracles!"

Throughout the tumultuous Covid era, I managed to steer clear of the illness. Frankly, I had my hands full already, thank you very much! Struggling with the isolating effects of Parkinson's, the additional layer of isolation imposed by the pandemic barely registered on my radar. Family gatherings persisted, conversations thrived via WhatsApp, bridging the physical distances between us and our beloved children and grandchildren. Reflecting, I shudder at the thought of navigating both Covid and Parkinson's simultaneously at that juncture in my life. I emerged unscathed from the pandemic, and for that, I am profoundly grateful.

Little did I foresee the impending shift in the tides. Around the second week of June 2023, Melinda tested positive for Covid, and her illness was severe. Despite our efforts to minimize contact, fate had other plans. On Father's Day, June 18, 2023, I received my own positive diagnosis for Covid—a blindsiding blow that left me reeling. I thought I knew exhaustion, courtesy of Parkinson's, but the sheer fatigue induced by Covid atop my existing battles caught me off guard. The debilitating weariness rendered me virtually immobile, struggling even to rise from my recliner for necessities. My body echoed with pains and aches of an intensity previously unknown to me. As sleep remained elusive, a new chapter of challenges unfolded, testing my resilience to its limits. Adding to the mix of sleeplessness, a prominent symptom of Parkinson's, I found myself in such a pit of despair that I yearned for the simpler days when Parkinson's was my sole adversary!

After enduring the throes of illness for a couple of weeks, I emerged utterly drained. Seeking solace, I visited my family physician, a man of faith whose words never fail to uplift my spirits. I recounted my Covid ordeal, seeking guidance on the road to recovery.

His response struck me like a bolt of lightning. "Given your ongoing battle with Parkinson's, your recovery from Covid may span anywhere from six months to two years," he explained. "I suggest sticking to your current routine and gradually reintroducing exercise. Strengthening your body and bolstering your immune system will be key."

Ugh. Not quite the prognosis I had hoped for. Despite my reluctance, I sluggishly eased back into a fitness regimen, aiming for four thirty-minute workouts per week. I planned to supplement this routine with my usual biweekly ritual of two-hour sessions on the lawnmower

By mid-July, Oklahoma was in the throes of one of the most scorching heat waves I had ever experienced! Venturing out to prepare the mower post-Covid, the suffocating heat overwhelmed my lungs, nearly sending me reeling. The untamed corners awaiting the mower's touch—fence lines, the sprawling pond, and the mystical Forest of Bren—were resigned to their overgrown fate throughout July and August.

The summer of 2023 unfurled in relentless waves of sweltering heat, rendering me incapable of tackling any outdoor tasks for several weeks. The trifecta of Parkinson's, Covid, and scorching heat left me so drained and debilitated that I couldn't muster the strength to serenade the keys of the piano or belt out a tune, leading us to unprecedentedly cancel our Wednesday night church gatherings for a whole month. A rare occurrence in our household, to say the least.

As it turns out, there's genuine merit in honoring the rest our bodies crave. There's wisdom in granting oneself the grace to recuperate and recharge the soul's batteries. Each day, I consciously chose rest, shed any guilt associated with downtime, embraced the essence of living, and found joy in simply existing.

"I never lose sight of the fact that just being is fun," as Katharine Hepburn aptly put it.

Embracing the joy of living daily shed light on a profound realization—I, an introvert by nature, thrive in solitude, a sentiment not shared by my dear wife! True living, I learned, unfolds in the tapestry of relationships. Despite my inclination toward solitude, the weeks of reprieve underscored a deeper need for human connection over isolation. Following the hiatus from our Wednesday night worship gatherings, Melinda and I mutually agreed (she might have nudged me a bit...) that our souls craved communal fellowship.

As the summer heat gradually subsided, allowing us to breathe freely in the outdoors once more, we revived our Wednesday evening worship gatherings, witnessing a revival of life and vigor coursing through our beings!

On August 22, 2023, a routine visit to my optometrist took an unexpected turn when I was informed of cataracts clouding my vision, necessitating lens replacement surgery for both eyes.

In early September, I underwent surgery on my left eye. The day before, during the eye exam, I couldn't even read the largest letters. Post-surgery, to my amazement, I could effortlessly decipher the tiniest script. Two weeks later, the right eye underwent the same transformative surgery, yielding identical results. The extent of my deteriorated vision had eluded me until then. Following each surgery, a bedtime ritual involved donning an eye patch for slumber, a detail I casually shared with my barber. Misinterpreting the instructions, she humorously inquired how I managed to scribble away with a patch covering my eye. My playful response? "Just like a pirate!"

Reflecting on these twists and turns, I am reminded of the importance of maintaining a structured routine while allowing room for spontaneous bursts of creativity and play. Those "I didn't see that coming" moments are an inevitable part of life's tapestry. Embracing flexibility and patience, viewing such surprises through the lens of faith, sustains me. Yet, adhering to a weekly regimen provides anticipation and purpose. Vision, in both the literal and metaphorical sense, fuels hope and fortitude. It propels me to compose music, pen books and blogs, and extend my ministry to others. Vision breathes life into my days, painting a canvas of possibilities and offering solace in the face of life's unexpected curveballs.

NINETEEN
PROOF GOD LOVES ME

"We take ourselves way too seriously, and we don't take God seriously enough. It is not by accident that humor and humility come from the same root word. If you can laugh at yourself, you'll always have plenty of good material."

— RICK WARREN

I've recognized a nagging sense that time is slipping away, leaving me scrambling to immortalize my thoughts for my family's posterity. I teeter on the brink of burnout, merely skimming the surface of life without truly relishing the essence of existence. The tipping point arrived after a midweek church gathering in our cozy living room, where a friend's astute observation struck a chord.

Prompted by her insight, I mustered the courage to shoot her a candid text the following day: "Last night, your parting words about self-care lingered in my mind. I value your perspective and seek your guidance on how

I can better nurture myself. Any suggestions you have are most welcome. Just striving to steward my body well."

Her swift reply encapsulated a wealth of wisdom: "Acknowledge your physical boundaries and operate within them, rather than incessantly pushing against them. Ease up on the mental gymnastics. Allow your mind and body moments of respite. It seems like you're always sprinting the marathon at full throttle, burdening yourself with towering expectations. No groundbreaking wisdom here. Embrace moments of stillness before the divine. My prayers accompany you unfailingly."

Her words hit home. I grapple with my physical constraints instead of embracing them. Every thought is dissected to the minutest detail. I feel like a burden unless I'm immersed in ceaseless productivity or creativity. My wife's gentle reminders to slow down and unwind resound continuously but implementing them remains a Herculean task. As I pen these words, physical and mental fatigue weigh me down. However, amidst the weariness, a particular scripture passage urges me not to rush through life, but to savor moments of pure existence.

> "Are you tired? Worn out? Burned out on religion? Come to me. Get away with me and you'll recover your life. I'll show you how to take a real rest. Walk with me and work with me—watch how I do it. Learn the unforced rhythms of grace. I won't lay anything heavy or ill-fitting on you. Keep company with me and you'll learn to live freely and lightly."
>
> — JESUS, MATTHEW 11:28-30 (THE MESSAGE)

PARKINSON'S & RECREATION 2

One thing that constantly resonates in my thoughts as a gentle nudge to embrace the present is the unwavering love of God. His love knows no bounds—it envelops me in moments of triumph, in bouts of foul moodiness, in times of blunders, and in moments of vulnerability. His love holds me close, tenderly guiding me toward growth.

Through the profound love of Jesus Christ, I've found the capacity to extend forgiveness effortlessly to those who inflict wounds and to chuckle at my own mishaps, finding joy in life's simple pleasures, even in the face of Parkinson's. As this chapter unfolds, I'll share a couple of memories that underscore the depth of God's love for me and hopefully will lift your spirits. Let's kick off with a gem:

Every December, for years, my dear friend Matt and I went to Tulsa for a festive shopping spree to pick out Christmas gifts for our better halves. Stepping foot in a sprawling mall one day, I quipped, "I hope I go incognito today."

No sooner had the words left my lips than a familiar voice called out, "Matt! How's it going?"

Matt affably connected with everyone he met, creating instant camaraderie. It felt like a reunion of long-lost pals at every turn. This scenario played out multiple times during that mall excursion, granting me a blissful sense of anonymity and carefree wandering. I jestingly remarked, "Looks like you're the celebrity today, Matt! No one notices me."

We shared hearty chuckles each time someone intercepted us, with me teasing Matt about his newfound fame. Amidst our shopping spree, Matt suggested a pit stop at Victoria's Secret—where he always picked out something special for his beloved. Feeling like a fish out of water in the lingerie section, I swiftly embraced the absurdity by playfully brandishing various pieces of delicate undergarments, hollering across the store, "Hey, Matt! How about this one?"

With each brazen display, the antics escalated until I triumphantly hoisted a pair of ruby red, lacy panties aloft, teasingly asking, "Matt! What's the verdict on THESE?"

Amidst my impromptu fashion show, a tap on my shoulder jolted me back to reality. "Excuse me, aren't you Dennis Jernigan, the musician?" a woman asked. "The worship leader?"

A crimson blush engulfed me as I sheepishly confirmed my identity, the embarrassment radiating from me like the vivid hue of the panties I clutched. "Yes, that's me," I muttered, wishing I could fade into the ground. But oh no, my foot wasn't done digging its own grave—I felt compelled to offer an explanation, blurting out, "I'm just assisting my friend with his gift selection for his wife." My attempt at clarifying matters only made things more awkward.

> "Laughter is a holy thing. It is as sacred as music and silence and solemnity, maybe more sacred. Laughter is like a prayer, like a bridge over which creatures tiptoe to meet each other. Laughter is like mercy; it heals. When you can laugh at yourself, you are free."
>
> — TED LODER.

PARKINSON'S & RECREATION 2

Some of life's greatest joys and belly laughs often induce a cringe in my children. As detailed in my earlier work on Parkinson's, my rural upbringing has instilled in me a penchant for embracing nature in its purest form—nudity included. It's not uncommon for me to saunter out the back door, sans clothing, to one of my designated spots for a leisurely bathroom break off the back deck. One fateful day, as I roamed the house in my birthday suit, my son Ezra stumbled upon the sight, exclaiming, "Dad! Put some clothes on!"

I quipped back, "This is my domain! Feel free to vacate!" His mortified expression clashed with my unbridled sense of freedom, basking in the simple pleasure of being one with nature. In that moment, I sensed a divine chuckle resonating within me, a gentle reminder of unconditional love amidst life's quirky adventures.

As much as these tales evoke joy and a sense of love within me, there's an equal, if not greater, number of profound and sacred instances that affirm my belief in God's affection toward me. These are the moments where I sense not just love but a genuine fondness, a feeling that God not only loves me but also enjoys my company and presence.

TWENTY
WHEN LIFE IS ALTERED

"It may be hard for an egg to turn into a bird: it would be a jolly sight harder for it to learn to fly while remaining an egg. We are like eggs at present. And you cannot go on indefinitely being just an ordinary, decent egg. We must be hatched or go bad."

— C. S. LEWIS

Michael J. Fox is one of the most influential advocates for Parkinson's awareness and research funding, having raised over 2 billion dollars toward finding a cure. His journey began amidst the glitz of Hollywood, where he rose to stardom with iconic roles in the hit sitcom "Family Ties" and the beloved "Back to the Future" film trilogy. However, during his Hollywood days, around 1988, a subtle twitch in his pinkie signaled the onset of Parkinson's disease, altering the course of his life.

My admiration for Michael J. Fox remains unwavering. He has battled Parkinson's since the tender age of 29 and continues to bravely confront the disease at 63, marking 34 years of resilience. In a poignant documentary released in 2023, Michael candidly shared his journey with Parkinson's, shedding light on the realities of living with the condition. A striking moment arose when he opened up about the intensity of his pain, likening each tremor to a seismic upheaval. Reflecting on his experience, Michael revealed, "It's not so much pain from the movement, but from the not moving."

> "We must embrace pain and burn it as fuel for our journey."
>
> — KENJI MIYAZAWA

I find a deep resonance with Michael's story, particularly in navigating a life trajectory vastly different from my aspirations. The initial disorientation and faith-testing moments following my own diagnosis mirror the challenges he has courageously faced.

Navigating the realm of faith and personal identity amidst the challenges of Parkinson's disease or any other life-altering condition can be a profound journey. Parkinson's has led me to question my identity in a whole new light, casting shadows on my ability to embrace roles like being a husband, a father, a grandfather, or simply a man.

The disease's relentless grip has at times left me feeling stripped of my sense of self, waging a silent battle against my physical and mental well-being. Yet, amidst the struggles, a flicker of hope emerged when the Lord intervened in a remarkable way. Despite the sleepless nights that Parkinson's often brings, I've come to view these moments as opportunities for divine connections. One such poignant instance unfolded on the morning of August 16, 2023, as I lay awake in the early hours, opting to seek solace in God's presence instead of reaching for sleep aids. To my surprise, the musings of a new song flowed effortlessly onto my iPhone notes, a gentle reminder that even in the darkness of night, divine inspiration can illuminate the soul.

Parkinson's has a way of cloaking me in a shroud of isolation and self-doubt, painting a distorted picture of reality. However, the truth lies in the unwavering support of my loving family and friends, offering solace in times of need. Yet, pride often creeps in, nudging me toward self-imposed seclusion, especially when the tremors in my right hand and arm draw unwanted attention in public settings. The urge to conceal these visible signs of the disease becomes a vicious cycle of anxiety and self-consciousness, hindering genuine connections with others.

In these moments, I unintentionally retreat into a shell, contrary to the essence of true life found in meaningful relationships, unaffected by Parkinson's tremors. Those who truly care for me see beyond the physical manifestations of the disease, embracing me unconditionally, tremor and all. The unwavering love and support of my dear ones serve as pillars of strength in my journey with Parkinson's. Through the heartfelt lyrics of my latest creation, "I'm Still Here," I aim to offer a glimpse into my personal struggles and the resilient spirit that guides me. Crafted in the quiet whispers of the night, this song serves as a raw reflection of my innermost thoughts and a heartfelt plea to my Father in heaven.

I'm Still Here
Words & Music: Dennis Jernigan
Received on: August 16, 2023

Verse 1:
Sometimes I get so overwhelmed
By the simple things of life
Sometimes people avoid me
I can see it in their eyes
Sometimes my heart's so shaken
As I watch the world go by
Like I have already died
Sometimes I get discouraged
By the storm surrounding me
Sometimes I shut out loved ones
'Cause I don't want them to see
Sometimes I lose sight of who I am and used to be
But deep inside I'm still just me

(The first half of the chorus is a declaration:)
I'm still here
Caught between the joy and pain
I'm still here
Between the desert and the rain
I'm still here
Just out of reach, yet feel love's flame
I'm still here
Explainable yet unexplained

PARKINSON'S & RECREATION 2

(The second half of the chorus is me crying out to God:)
Just be near
Bringing joy to comfort pain
Just be near
Cool the desert with Your rain
Just be near
Come consume me in love's flame
Just be near
When my life goes unexplained
Just be near
Just be near

Verse 2:
Sometimes I get so caught up
In the me, myself, and I
I become a desert island
Left there wondering why
I can choose the darkness
Or can choose to walk in Light
I choose joy and I choose life

Repeat Chorus

©2023 Shepherd's Heart Music, Inc.
Dennisjernigan.com • 800-877-0406
Administered by PraiseCharts.com

As I battle Parkinson's, Melinda and I often share a simple yet profound message of hope: "As long as you're breathing, there is hope." Despite the challenges that

Parkinson's presents to my physical and mental well-being, I have made a conscious choice to embrace each day with joy, irrespective of how I may feel. Refusing to let my emotions define me, I channel my feelings into prayer.

> "Resilience is all about being able to overcome the unexpected. Sustainability is about survival. The goal of resilience is to thrive."
>
> — JAMES CASCIO

James Cascio's words echo a sentiment close to my heart, that resilience isn't just about surviving, it's about thriving in the face of adversity. Even in moments of pain, I find solace in turning to God and cherishing precious moments with my wife and family. Surrounded by those who love me unconditionally, the veil of pain often lifts, giving way to moments of pure joy. Despite the altered circumstances that Parkinson's has brought into my life, I've discovered a newfound appreciation for the beauty of life and a deeper sense of gratitude than I ever imagined.

TWENTY-ONE
GAMES WITH GRANDSONS

I firmly believe that creativity is a divine gift bestowed upon us by God. As beings made in His image, creativity is inherently woven into our essence. To me, creativity means having the ability to perceive life and its complexities through the lens of God's perspective. This outlook keeps me open and eager to be inspired in the most unexpected and delightful ways.

Recently, a moment of creative inspiration amusingly unfolded in a playful dispute between three of my grandsons. It began when Melinda and I invited our three eldest grandsons for a Friday night stay, planning to watch the classic Alfred Hitchcock film, *The Birds*. We thought it would be a fun way to bond with the boys and observe their reactions to suspenseful situations. Their youthful bravado was evident as they confidently proclaimed, "How scary can a movie about birds be?"

During the movie screening, our brave trio of warriors (aged 8, 9, and 10) displayed moments of feigned fear, peeking through their fingers while pretending not to be scared. Despite their attempts to be fearless, their animated reactions never failed to entertain me. Their witty banter and keen observations always brought a touch of humor to the experience. I'll spare you the intricate details of their commentary, but let's just say discussions revolved around the movie's visual effects and the ongoing blue screen versus green screen debate in filmmaking—a true reflection of the CGI era we live in!

Before the movie night, I had taken the boys to the Forest of Bren for a game of hide and seek. Giving them a five-minute head start, I navigated the forest in a John Deere Gator, attempting to track them down. While I managed to capture one of the boys (mainly because he opted for a ride instead of running), the other two cunningly eluded me and triumphantly reached the forest's entrance, claiming victory. Their joy and excitement were palpable, prompting us to plan another round of the game for the following day.

The following day, my grandsons proposed a role reversal—grandpa hiding in the forest while they took on the challenge of finding me. Giving me a purported five-minute head start (though it felt more like a mere moment), I swiftly made my way to a secluded trail nestled between two main paths before their quest began. With a simple strategy in mind (keep silent and make a stealthy return to the forest's entrance to reclaim the Gator), I settled on the damp forest floor, clad in neon yellow and orange gloves that inadvertently made me stand out, a detail that Parkinson's subtly made known due to its telltale tremors. The struggle of staying perfectly still with Parkinson's? Well, let's just say it's an uphill battle.

PARKINSON'S & RECREATION 2

Amid hushed whispers and the gentle rustling of leaves, I observed with amusement as each boy cautiously tread closely, their determination palpable. Suppressing the urge to burst into laughter, I prayed that my involuntary movements wouldn't betray me before their watchful eyes. Once confident that they had ventured deep into the forest, I stealthily rose from my concealment, made my way to the Gator, revved up the engine, and boisterously declared, "Grandpa wins!"

In a matter of seconds, the boys dashed back to the Gator, eager to uncover my hiding spot, a secret I cunningly withheld for future games. After all, a strategic advantage never hurt anyone, right? Their infectious laughter mingled with the thrill of the chase inspired me to suggest a game of capture the flag. Dividing into teams, the older boys formed one alliance while my 8-year-old grandson and I joined forces on the opposing side. In the absence of real flags, my neon gloves served as makeshift markers, adding a whimsical touch to our impromptu forest escapade.

Setting the stage, I established the rules for our spirited game of capture the flag. The 9- and 10-year-old boys were tasked with concealing their flag in the southern expanse of the forest, near the Gator, while my 8-year-old grandson and I strategically placed our flag in the northern domain, close to the legendary Bigfoot. The objective was clear: Retrieve the opposing team's flag and reach the forest entrance first to win.

As we ventured to the northern realms and secured our flag in position, I initiated the game with a distinctive call to action, echoing through the forest with a spirited "Hootie Hoo! Hootie Hoo!"

However, before I could even ignite the Gator's engine, a sudden proclamation disrupted the anticipated excitement. One of the boys from the opposing team boldly declared, "I quit!"

Unwilling to accept defeat so easily, I firmly asserted, "There is no quitting!" Yet, the resolute voice rang out once more, repeating the declaration of surrender. Reluctantly, I summoned all the boys to gather on the trail to address the unexpected turn of events.

As the two older boys approached, visibly agitated, I sensed the undercurrent of frustration and anger that colored the atmosphere. Eager to unearth the cause of my grandson's decision to bow out of the game, I prompted him to share his perspective. His explanation shed light on a tale of conflicting strategies, with he and his cousin at odds over the flag's burial location—a dispute fueled by differing interpretations of my instructions. Expressing his frustration, my grandson revealed, "He wanted to bury it close to the Gator, but I thought it should be placed slightly further away, as you said 'in the vicinity' of the alligator, not right next to it."

Turning to his cousin for clarification, I sought his side of the story. He defended his stance by emphasizing the practicality of burying the flag closer to the alligator for easier retrieval, sparking a clash of opinions that escalated into mutual exasperation. The crux of the matter rested on a nuanced understanding of my directive, as the cousin asserted, "Grandpa never said we couldn't

PARKINSON'S & RECREATION 2

bury the flag. I saw it as our ticket to victory and wanted to seize the opportunity to win."

As the standoff continued, I felt fatigued, both physical and mental, exacerbated by the challenges of Parkinson's. Seeking divine guidance for a solution, I silently implored the Lord for wisdom and harmony in the face of discord and a revelation soon unfolded.

Guided by a higher wisdom, I tapped into the boys' innate desire for honor and camaraderie, aiming to bridge the chasm of contention with words of empathy and insight. Addressing the trio, I posed a poignant question, "What holds greater value—triumph in the game or nurturing a bond of love and respect with your cousin?" The query lingered in the air, met with a palpable silence tinged with lingering frustration.

In a bid to steer the conversation toward reconciliation, I probed further, "Is it preferable to stand by your convictions or prioritize fostering a loving relationship with your cousin?"

The boy on the brink of quitting staunchly defended his standpoint, asserting, "But I know I'm right."

Sensing an opportunity for a deeper reflection, I challenged him with a hypothetical scenario: "How would your coach react if you expressed the intention to abandon the team?" His response, clouded by indignation, hinted at a lingering defiance, countered by my unwavering stance on the importance of loyalty and commitment, especially in the heat of competition.

Facing a waning reserve of energy, I peeled back the layers of my vulnerability to reveal a poignant truth—the irreplaceable loss of two cousins during the pandemic, a poignant reminder of missed opportunities for heartfelt farewells. Expressing the ache of separation and the yearning for closure, I shared my regret at not being able to convey my love to them one last time, a sentiment that transcended the trivialities of a game.

As the weight of my words settled upon the boys, a subtle thawing of resentment gave way to a shared understanding of loss and longing. Embracing the moment of vulnerability, I underscored the essence of our connection, emphasizing that amidst the trials of Parkinson's, the bond forged in shared experiences and cherished memories far outweighed the allure of victory in a fleeting contest.

As I uttered those heartfelt words, tears welled up uncontrollably, a testament to the depth of my emotions as I bared my soul to the boys. I painted a vivid picture of love and sacrifice, emphasizing how their squabbles pained me deeply. I professed my unwavering devotion, willing to lay down my life for them in a heartbeat. The vulnerability in my voice struck a chord, evoking a shared cascade of tears streaming down their cheeks.

Steering the conversation toward reconciliation once more, I reiterated the pivotal question, "What truly holds greater significance—the pursuit of victory or nurturing bonds of kinship with your cousin?" With a heartfelt prayer for grace and understanding, I implored the heavens for guidance in fostering forgiveness and love amidst disagreements.

Closing the poignant moment with an earnest "Amen," I entrusted the older boys with the task of resolving their differences, urging them to seek common

PARKINSON'S & RECREATION 2

ground before reuniting at the forest entrance. Turning to my young teammate, brimming with renewed resolve, I rallied us to resume our quest for the elusive flag with zeal and determination. After a fruitless search yielded no results, we returned to find the older boys engaged in jovial banter, a heartening sign of reconciliation.

Prompting them about the resolution of their dispute, I was met with affirmative nods, signaling a restored harmony between the once-estranged cousins. With a playful quip, I teased them about the cryptic clue they left behind, a pile of sticks serving as a whimsical marker for our hidden flag. Chuckling at the clever ruse, I playfully chided, "You claimed it was 'in the vicinity of the alligator' and here we are, decoding stick formations as clues!" Their laughter echoed through the forest.

It warms my heart to share that both boys extended the olive branch of forgiveness, separately approaching me with words that resonated deep within my soul, "I really love you, Grandpa." In that poignant moment, a wave of fulfillment washed over me, infusing me with renewed strength to cherish our time together as we ventured deeper into the forest's embrace.

Guided by a shared sense of reconciliation, we cleared the trails of branches and debris, a symbolic act of preparing the path for future adventures with their siblings. Observing them tackle the tasks at hand with a maturity beyond their years, I marveled at the sight of these young souls embodying selfless love and dedication, all while radiating a contagious joy that uplifted our spirits.

I witnessed their transformation from boys to young men, embodying duty, camaraderie and family.

TWENTY-TWO
'I ONLY NEED SODA WATER AND MY DADA'

"There are only two lasting bequests we can hope to give our children. One of these is roots, the other, wings."

— JOHANN WOLFGANG VON GOETHE

The profound impact of my grandchildren's words and antics amazes me. Each quip or gesture has the power to momentarily lift the veil of Parkinson's, granting me respite and rejuvenating my spirit. Their presence is a soothing balm for my soul. So, get ready for a joyride as I share snippets of my favorite quotes from these little bundles of sunshine. Their infectious charm and wisdom are bound to brighten your day!

Theodore, the 4-year-old meltdown maestro, declared, "I only need soda water and my dada!"—a classic moment of toddler drama that probably resonates with anyone who has experienced a little one's emotional outburst.

Onto the tale of Theo and the lucky Texas Rangers hat —a cherished piece from my ball cap collection that found its rightful owner in Theo. Fast forward to the year the Rangers clinched the World Series title, and there's Theo proudly sporting the hat. When reminded by his mom, Raina, that the hat was a gift from grandpa, Theo's quick retort, "I was already thinking of Grandpa!" melted my heart and painted a smile on my face that lasted all day.

Next up, we have little Edison's mischievous suggestion to his mom while driving: "Mom, let go of the handle and see what happens!" A moment of spontaneous humor that had my daughter texting me in amusement, knowing it's the quirky antics of my grandkids that keep my spirits high daily.

Zella, the 6-year-old bundle of joy, brought a tear to my eye in her one-of-a-kind endearing way. Zella, during a medical visit with her mom, playfully wiggled her hand when asked to hold it still, proclaiming it as her "party hand." Her endearing mimicry of my own hand tremor touches me deeply, reinforcing the special bond we share.

We honestly never know what to expect to come out of our grandchildren's mouths and they never fail to brighten our days! Cullen, Annē's 10-year-old, during a memorable car ride on the way home from a memorial service, asked his mom, "What is your greatest fear?"

She answered, "Losing you or one of your brothers or your sister."

He replied, "Mine would be elevators." LOL!

Now, let's turn our attention to Ronald, the 8-year-old prankster with a heart of gold. During a visit, he wasted no time enlisting my help for a mischievous prank involving police crime scene tape. I played along, transforming into a mock murder victim on the porch, complete with a theatrical pose and a dose of humor. He stood beside me after wrapping me up and I put my glasses askew on my face and slumped my head over on my right shoulder with my mouth agape and my tongue hanging out. I asked my son, Ezra, to take a picture of the murder scene. He got out his phone and took a picture, but then said, "You're not dead yet. You're still moving," referring to the tremor in my party hand.

I said, "That's just the nerves reacting involuntarily to my death, like the way a lizard's severed tail keeps on writhing after it has broken off!" Dad humor at its finest.

Ron, with a penchant for Church's Chicken, unwittingly provided comic relief during a church service by associating the word "church" with his favorite fast-food joint. In August 2023, while sitting in a church service, Ron wanted to stay with his mom in the "big" service. Pastor McCracken was preaching about the church and asked people what their first thought was when they hear the word "church."

Ron yelled out, "Chicken!" His mom clamped her hand over his mouth "What?" he laughed. "I like Church's Chicken!"

When my children were young, I intentionally sang them to sleep almost every night, and I am glad to say that my children tend to carry on the tradition with their own children. Annē, serenading 5-year-old Zella at bedtime, captured a delightful family group chat voice recording. However, the bedtime serenade sparked a touch of jealousy in 6-year-old Harry, who felt left out. Quick to remedy the situation, Annē invited Harry to his bed for a personalized lullaby session. Harry was so excited as soothing tunes filled the room. After a couple of songs, Harry, in his candid manner, declared, "OK. That's enough," bringing a chuckle to everyone's lips.

TWENTY-THREE
MORE PROOF GOD LOVES ME

I am reminded of the moments where God's love and presence surprised me in extraordinary ways. One memory takes me back to 2009 in Belo Horizonte, Brazil, where a worship conference awaited me as a guest speaker and worship leader. Expecting a church gymnasium setting familiar to an American, imagine my shock as we drove up to a soccer stadium with over 25,000 attendees. The scale of the gathering was truly breathtaking.

My admiration for Keith Green's ministry runs deep, stemming from the impactful concert he held at Oklahoma Baptist University in 1978, which introduced me to contemporary Christian music. His influence was so profound that I found myself honing Keith Green piano melodies over classical compositions. The tragic loss of Keith and two of his children, Bethany and Josiah, resonated with me. Visiting Keith's resting place, where he cradles his children in eternal peace, became a poignant moment I cherished. Melody, Keith's wife, went on to write Keith's amazing biography, *No Compromise*, which helped me tremendously in my own struggles. She became a hero to me. I never expected to meet her in this life.

The unexpected encounter with Melody Green at a Christian Booksellers Association convention in Orlando, Florida, in 1998 was a surreal experience. While signing my latest book and recording, Melody passed by, stirring a mix of disbelief and excitement. Seizing the opportunity, I excused myself from a fan's book signing, declaring, "One of my heroes is walking by, and I must meet her!"

Embarking on a somewhat awkward yet thrilling encounter, I found myself clumsily approaching Melody Green, my words tumbling out in a rush. "Melody, the ministry of you and your husband has radically altered my life forever, and I wanted to say thank you in person."

Her gracious response and immediate inquiry about my identity caught me off guard. As I began introducing myself, she eagerly interjected, "Dennis Jernigan?! I've been wanting to meet you!" The disbelief and joy in that moment made me feel like I had stepped into a heavenly realm. This impromptu meeting with Melody was a dream come true, bridging the gap between admiration and reality in a serendipitous moment.

A pivotal moment in my life unfolded on November 7, 1981, during a concert by the Christian band, 2nd Chapter of Acts. Annie Herring, the lead singer, paused to share a message from the Lord that resonated deeply with me, transforming my very being. It took me seven years to muster the courage to share this profound experience with others. I held a fervent desire to personally express my gratitude to the members of 2nd Chapter of Acts, praying for an opportunity to do so.

By 1988, my life had undergone a radical transformation, embracing marriage and parenthood. Initiating a monthly worship gathering called The Night of Praise in 1985, I extended an invitation to Annie Herring to lead worship, hoping to convey my heartfelt appreciation for her role in my spiritual journey. The shock of her acceptance was surpassed only by the joy of not only thanking her in person but also sharing a duet of her iconic song, "Easter Song." Over the years, our paths intertwined through concerts, album collaborations, and a touching request from Annie to record one of my songs. The overwhelming sense of being divinely loved in these encounters with one of my faith heroes leaves me in awe.

As 1988 rolled in, the disbandment of 2nd Chapter of Acts left me with a tinge of disappointment, fearing I might never have the chance to express my gratitude to the other two members, Nelly Greisen and Matthew Ward. The longing to thank Annie's siblings for their impact on my life lingered. Fast forward to 1989, where an opportunity arose at a James Robison Bible Conference in Fort Worth, Texas, before a crowd of 15,000 attendees. Amidst the bustling scene, including a concert by renowned Christian artist Mylon LeFevre, a fateful encounter unfolded backstage with a man named Steve Greisen. Inquiring about a possible connection to Nelly Greisen, his response, "She's my wife," set the stage for a heartfelt revelation of how her ministry had changed my life. Little did I know that this encounter would pave the way for yet another divine rendezvous. Moments later,

Steve introduced me to Nelly, and I poured out my heartfelt thanks for being a vessel of God's love in my life. Each serendipitous meeting with my faith heroes reaffirmed God's profound love for me.

Fast forward to 1995, as I geared up to record a live album at Christ for the Nations Institute in Dallas, Texas, when a thought flickered in my mind: "Wouldn't it be incredible if Matthew Ward could join me for a duet on this album?" Despite hearing about his battle with cancer, a friend's encouragement nudged me to reach out to Matthew.

His enthusiastic response of "Yes, I would love to record with you!" defied all expectations. This collaboration marked the beginning of a lasting friendship, with Matthew gracing my concerts, visiting my home, and contributing his talent to two more of my albums. The journey of meeting and thanking these faith luminaries underscored the depth of God's love and orchestration in my life.

Having my prayers answered in unexpected and profound ways across many years may not strike you as significant, but it is a testament to God's immense love for me. This unwavering belief fuels my resilience, fortitude, and sanity in the face of Parkinson's attempts to challenge or dim my faith in God's love. In the realm of His perfect love, fear finds no place to dwell.

And now, to wrap up this chapter, let's dive into a heartwarming text message I received from my son-in-law, Chip. At a religious gathering in Atlanta, Georgia, on May 12, 2022, Chip had a chance encounter with the renowned spiritual leader in the Christian faith, Louie

Giglio. In their conversation, when Chip mentioned my name, Louie's response was nothing short of touching: "Your father is a legend and very loved and respected."

Chip shared with me, "I was on the verge of tears meeting him." The sheer act of Chip passing on this heartfelt encounter speaks volumes. The knowledge of being cherished and living a life of purpose fills me with gratitude, serving as another testament to the overwhelming love that God showers upon me.

> "There is no fear in love, but perfect love drives out fear, because fear involves punishment, and the one who fears is not perfected in love."
>
> — 1 JOHN 4:18 (NASB)

TWENTY-FOUR
AUSSIE! AUSSIE! AUSSIE! OI! OI! OI!

Ah, the battle cry that separates the true-blue Aussies from the rest of us. As someone who's had the pleasure of immersion in the vibrant Australian culture, I've come to appreciate the unique way they communicate.

You see, when you're in a group of Aussies and you want to find the real deal, all you have to do is let out a rousing "Aussie! Aussie! Aussie!" and wait for the resounding "Oi! Oi! Oi!" in response. It's like a secret handshake, a way to identify your fellow countrymen (and women) in the most spirited fashion.

One of the delights of being in Australia with Melinda is watching her navigate the tricky waters of the local lingo. Our son-in-law, Ashley, will be deep in conversation, and suddenly Melinda will chime in, "I didn't understand a word you just said!"

This, of course, sends me into fits of laughter—the kind that start in the belly and bubble up until I'm in stitches. But it's a two-way street, as Ash has had to turn to me on more than one occasion and ask, "What did Mama J just say?" or "What does she mean by that?"

You see, Aussies have a way of turning the English language on its head. McDonald's becomes "Mackas," sunglasses are "sunnies," and breakfast is "brekkie." And the slang doesn't stop there. "Dinkum" or "fair dinkum" means something is true or genuine, "Chrissie" is Christmas, and "good onya" is a job well done. If someone "shouts ya," they're buying, and "heaps" means a whole lot of something. Candy is "lollies," potato chips are "crisps," and biscuits are "scones." French fries are "chips," cookies are "biscuits," and a gift is a "prezzie." And let's not forget the trusty "barbie" for a barbecue, "swimmers" for swimsuits, and a "jumper" for a sweater. Ah, the rich tapestry of Aussie culture. It's enough to make you want to shout, "Bob's your uncle!" (which means "there you have it") as you bake up a batch of those "biscuits" in the oven. Oh, the world of the "tall poppies" in Australia—where successful people are celebrated, not shunned. And let's not forget the humble "thongs," which in Oz refer to those ubiquitous flip-flops, not the, well, shall we say, more intimate attire.

As an American in this vibrant land, I've had to learn a few things the hard way. For instance, the term "fanny" has a rather vulgar connotation, so it's best to avoid wearing those "fanny packs" while in Australia. And then there was the time I innocently observed our newborn granddaughter, Elliott, "rooting around" for her mother's breast, only to be quickly enlightened that "rooting around" is Aussie slang for something much more... amorous.

PARKINSON'S & RECREATION 2

Trying to keep track of all the slang can be a real "head trip" for this American with Parkinson's. "Awkie" means "awkward"—and believe me, I've felt that way more than a few times during a recent three-week stay.

But the true joys of being in Australia go far beyond the linguistic challenges. Our Aussie kids have a pool nestled on a majestic hillside, overlooking a vast forest. The sounds of cockatoos, parakeets, and kookaburras create a Jurassic Park-esque ambiance as we swim in the summer sun—a stark contrast to the blizzards and ice storms back home in Oklahoma during that January.

And then there was the time the girls wanted to play "Marco Polo" in the pool. Little did I know, these Aussie kids are ruthless cheaters, opening their eyes underwater, thinking I couldn't see them. Ah, the trials and tribulations of being an American grandparent in the land of the "tall poppies" and "thongs."

Having been around the block a time or two with my own kids, I knew a thing or two about combating cheating in Marco Polo. So, when the girls wanted to play, I shared my secret weapon: a pair of swim goggles blacked out with duct tape. The designated "it" person would have to wear these special goggles, effectively cutting down on any sneaky peeking. We affectionately called this version "Real Man Marco Polo," and the girls were delighted by the idea (though little Tilly still managed to find ways to slyly slip the goggles up and get a sneaky glimpse).

But that wasn't the only trick I had up my sleeve. I also taught them the thrilling and hilarious "Silent Marco Polo"—where the people the "it" person is trying to catch must remain completely silent in the water. They can stand still or swim around stealthily, but not a peep is allowed. Let me tell you, the suspense is palpable!

The only word of caution I have for these amped-up versions of Marco Polo is to make sure the "it" person keeps their hands out in front of them at all times. We don't want any face-meets-pool-edge incidents, now do we?

Another blessing was watching my wife come alive with creative projects for our granddaughters. I can't help but cherish the memory of watching Melinda embrace her role as Aussie grandma. She's the craft queen, whipping up all sorts of imaginative creations for the girls' dollhouses, showcasing her knack for turning the most ordinary materials into extraordinary things. It's moments like these that make the occasional "oops" moments more endearing.

Leave it to Ash to plan the perfect birthday celebration for Hannah, even while we were all the way over in Australia! When the day arrived, the sudden influx of unfamiliar faces had my anxiety levels spiking. But I wasn't about to let Parkinson's ruin my daughter's special day. So, I quickly excused myself to take my meds and gather my thoughts.

That's when I noticed one of the guests, Phil, had come decked out in a vibrant Hawaiian shirt. Well, I just couldn't resist—I slipped on my own Hawaiian shirt and headed back to join the party. After all, when you've got at least one other guy rocking the tropical look, you know you're in good company. Safety in numbers and all that, right?

PARKINSON'S & RECREATION 2

As if the birthday festivities weren't enough, on another day Hannah and Ash also treated us to some of the best roast chicken the land Down Under had to offer. Just walking down the sidewalk, the mouthwatering aroma had my salivary glands working overtime. And when that feast was finally laid out before us, I could practically taste it with my eyes!

Everyone dug in eagerly, our conversation dissolving into a symphony of "yummy sounds." But as is often the case, my Parkinson's started to rear its head, causing my tremors to spike the moment I tried to wield a utensil. I even struggled to tear off a simple piece of chicken with my weakened hands. In that moment, I could feel myself starting to shut down, that familiar anxiety creeping back in as I worried all eyes were on me (which, of course, they weren't).

It didn't take long for my sweet Hannah to notice my struggle with the meal. Ever the perceptive one, she simply and quietly asked, "Dad, would you like some help cutting up your chicken?"

In that moment, I was instantly transported back to her childhood, memories of me cutting up her pancakes flooding my mind. The realization that we had now switched roles had me welling up with emotion. "I remember cutting up your pancakes for you when you were little...and now we've switched roles," I confessed, the poignancy of that moment hitting me hard.

But my dear Hannah and her family were there to support me every step of the way. After my admission that I needed help with the chicken, Elliott and Matilda jumped into action, their "care-for-G-Pa" radar blaring. I happened to be struggling with my socks one morning when they walked by, each girl snatching up a sock and declaring, "There! There, G Pa! We've got ya!" In those moments, I felt wonderfully weak, but even more wonderfully loved.

These types of incidental yet profoundly meaningful exchanges occurred frequently during our time in Australia. I know I'm probably sharing too much, but given this may be one of the last books I ever have the chance to write, I want to fill it with the good, the joyful, the memories that will stay with me forever. Even something as simple as Elliott's quip while we were watching *Percy Jackson*: "If Medusa was about to turn me into stone, I would get into a model pose so I would look good." Classic Elliott humor that had me chuckling.

The friendly competition was fierce during that backyard basketball game with Ash and his nephew Raiden. Try as we might, Team Parkinson's (that's me and Elliott) just couldn't pull out the win, falling short by a single measly point. As we made our way back to the house, I overheard Raiden boasting to his uncle, "I wasn't going to let an old man beat me!" Classic young buck trash talk.

Another memorable moment was when Ash asked about my Parkinson's diagnosis. I told him I was 59 years old, just 13 days shy of my 60th birthday, when I first received the news. Little Tilly then piped up, asking if kids could get Parkinson's too. I assured her it was incredibly rare and unlikely. That's when Ash got a mischievous glint in his eye, asking if I'd ever dabbled in parkour back in the day. "No, but you just gave me an idea for a Parkinson's business: Parkour for Parkinson's!" I exclaimed. The mental image of folks with Parkinson's leaping over obstacles and shuffling across various surfaces had me chuckling. Maybe he's onto something there!

Of course, no visit to Ash's would be complete without the girls' nightly goodnight routine. Each evening, Tilly would make the rounds, kissing her grandmother, her mother, and then finally whispering in my ear, "I saved the best for last." Cue the heart melting.

As bittersweet as it was, the time came for Melinda and me to load up our bags and head to the Sydney airport. Ash's parents, Terry and Annette, came out to see us off. Being grandparents themselves to kids living abroad, they understood all too well the difficulty of saying those goodbyes. As Terry embraced me, he squeezed tight and murmured through tears, "We understand. We understand." Annette mirrored the sentiment, making us feel so seen and loved, knowing our children would be in good hands even when we couldn't be there.

Saying goodbye to Hannah, Ash, Elliott, and Matilda at the Sydney airport was an emotional gut punch. Tears streaming, granddaughters clinging tightly, grandparents assuring them we'd see each other again soon. Melinda and I stood there in stunned silence, watching them disappear down the terminal, wondering when we'd have the chance to create more cherished memories together. Our fervent hope was that the countless joyful moments from the past 25 days would sustain them until our next reunion.

Of course, our trip couldn't end without a touch of unexpected hilarity. We've now dubbed it "The Wheelchair Incident." As I was being assisted onto the plane for our flight home, the wheelchair attendant took my backpack and secured it in the compartment below my seat. She then proceeded to push me down the jetway. In one horrifying instant, I heard her cry out "Oh no!" as my wheelchair suddenly careened down the sloped jetway, the poor attendant being dragged along. Thankfully, the chair was stopped when it hit the center rail. My backpack had come loose and caused the attendant to trip. Sheer terror was quickly followed by relief that no one was harmed. I apologized profusely, assuring the attendant I was fine and that it was my own fault for not securing the backpack properly. What a harrowing yet fitting bookend to our Aussie adventure!

Maybe I can add "wheelchair races down jetways" to the Parkour for Parkinson's business plan I pitched earlier. Lord knows I'll never forget those few heart-pounding seconds of pure terror. But at least I can look back on it all with a chuckle, the perfect punctuation mark on an unforgettable journey.

TWENTY-FIVE
MAD LIBS AND MORE GRANDKID MADNESS

Our grandson's 9th birthday bash took place at a local skating rink, where the kids were dropping like flies, many unfamiliar with the art of skating. Little Zella, our 5-year-old granddaughter, was having a tough time navigating the rink. In a moment of solidarity with a fallen comrade, she charmingly quipped, "Oh, you're as bad as me!"

My favorite quote from Ronald is, "I have so many regrets! I wish I had never done this!" After a tonsillectomy. He was 8 years old.

A few fun quotes from Matilda:
- "At school one time I accidentally spelled 'butt'...and 'boob.'"
- "He just said a swear word...why can't he just say 'oh sheeeee' or 'oh, shhhh.'"
- "Daddy, did you know animals have more bones than us?"

Ash, her dad: "That's nice."

"Okay. Hand me the controller!" Tilly replied.

- "Awww! A goat!!! Goats have such weird eyes."
- Matilda singing the lyrics of "Since You've Been Gone"…"I WISH YOU WERE GONE!"

Hannah, writing to her sister, Raina, "I was telling Elliott you had JBro CDs and were a fan and she just said, 'OMG! I get my love of them from her!'"

She loves Nick. For all you Boomers out there, JBros stands for Jonas Brothers.

From Hannah: "Matilda has been listening to Dad's music at bed, specifically his 'The Very First Christmas Tree' album (she's a massive fan). She just yelled out from her room, 'Mum, what does resin mean?' Hannah: 'Can you use it in a sentence?'

Matilda: 'Hold on!' (waits a few beats while listening to her song) 'Resin!' (Not helpful)

Hannah: 'It means plastic!'

Matilda: 'Okay, so plastic king!'

Hannah (LOL): 'The word is "risen"—like after Jesus rises from the dead!'

Matilda: 'Oh! That makes more sense.'"

Hannah wrote back a bit later to report, "[Tilly's] Now asleep dreaming about the plastic king…"

From Raina: "Edison kept asking Theo about his porcupine and we were all so confused. I then asked what he meant, and he said, 'The one from bubba's birthday!'

which we figured out was the pineapple. Theo suggested naming him Mr. Prickly."

Annē: "I let Zella be with me in church today and she sat in my lap, took my head in her hands and with tears in her eyes said 'I don't want you to die. I would miss you!' Like, what? I tried so hard not to laugh but I told her it's ok, people die, and I would miss her too, LOL!"

The Kay kids came over and I got too tired to play with them. As they were leaving, I told Cullen I was sorry I was a party pooper. He said, "You aren't a party pooper. You ARE the party!" Made my day.

Chip, Theo's dad, asked, "What do you want to do for work, Theo?"
"I want to do what you do and work where you work, dad."
Theo asked, "What about you, Edison?"
"I want to poop in your pants," replied Edison.

"While sitting in the car line for drop off at school today, Zella rolled down the window and asked if she could howl at the moon. Now the kids are fighting over who can howl at the moon."

Zella: "Mom…you know bees make honey? So we should pray for them, just so you know."

Zella, while watching "Tangled," said, "I wish I could have magic tears when someone dies so I can revive them."

"Zella just said, 'Mom, when I grow up, I'm gonna work at Alpine Medical with you!"
Harry chimed in, 'Why? She's gonna be too old to work with you!'"

Edison after his nap (still very sleepy), whispered, "Dada can I tell you something in your ear?"
"What is it?" (whispering even quieter)
"Dada…poop in your pants! Hehehehe!"

A conversation between brothers, Theodore (4) and Edison (2): Theodore asked, "Momma, why is dada not coming? I need my precious dada."
Edison's response? "He's not precious, he's a boy!"

"Theo gave Edison the rest of his Oreos after dinner just because, he's older now, so I gave him the rest of mine."

Theo, then 4 years old, asked his cousin Mark to play with him.
Mark asked, "What are you playing?"
Theo responded, "Something that doesn't mess up my hair."

Black Bear Bonanza 2024, Branson, Missouri: Theo woke up at 1 a.m. fully dressed and ready to go, shoes, hat, everything. Then he woke up at 5:45, still fully clothed and asked, "Why is it taking so long for everyone to get up?"

Edison: "When I pee…it's like soy sauce!"

Raina: "Theo also saw an old man walk in front of him at the dentist and leaned over and said, 'he's died' (like he's dead). Bahahaha! I was like, 'No, he is a normal living human that just happens to be old.'"

From her mom, Glory: "Annabell worked on creating a store last night. It looked like a shrine to me. She even had a sign for the front of the store. The sign read, 'Store and Grave prices are below.' I asked her if she meant to spell 'gravy' and she said, 'No, it's a grave. Remember I'm a chef and my daughter died?'" Quite the backstory for a general store!

Around the same time, Annabell's mom overheard Annabell talking to a Barbie: "Hey Barbie, I couldn't talk earlier because my throat hurt and I'm sick. Yeah, I can talk now."

"Recently, while I was having a conversation with Annabell about being content and obedient, she came up with the perfect response. 'You get what you get and don't throw a fit.'"

From Annabell's mom: "I wanted you to know when Annabell reads your daily devotions at the end when you write, 'DJ Zephaniah 3:17', she reads it out and pronounces it 'Zephaliath.'"

Annabell's mom said to her, "Uncle Chip has a snack for you." Annabell answered, "I hope it doesn't have peas." A girl after my own heart!

Gi Gi, My mom, told Zella she didn't want to get her make-up for her birthday, and Zella said, "That's Ok. I'll take dollars."

Raina: "I was telling Theo and Edison that I've eaten alligator and then Edison said, 'I want to rope one up and eat it with Dad.'"

Something I always find hilarious is the way young children pronounce words. Following are a few examples from my grandchildren's minds as sent to me by their parents:
Edison says "biguana" (iguana) and it's my favorite.
Theo and Edison also both say "muh-rote" instead of remote.
In the summer of 2023, Melinda and I drove two hours to Arkansas with two of our grandchildren to watch another grandchild perform a musical number with her summer camp members. Mark (8) and Annabell (5) wanted to play Mad Libs, a game we had played hundreds of times with our own children on the many road trips we took while they were growing up.
In Mad Libs, the underlined words are the blanks you have to fill in either with a noun, verb, adverb, a person's

PARKINSON'S & RECREATION 2

name, historical figure, etc. Those underlined words came from the minds of my grandchildren! You'll get the idea, lol!

Mad Libs:
Favorite Christmas Carols
Here's a list of the top 10 most <u>poopily</u> played Christmas carols.
Which one is your favorite?
1. "The Christmas Song" ("Chestnuts <u>Singing and Dancing</u> on a <u>Skinny</u> Fire")
2. "Have Yourself a Merry <u>Smelly</u> Christmas"
3. "<u>Fishgut</u> Wonderland"
4. "<u>Taylor Swift</u> Is Coming to Town"
5. "<u>Black</u> Christmas"
6. "Let It <u>Poop</u>"
7. "Jingle <u>Cow Poop</u> Rock"
8. "Little Drummer <u>Pee</u>"
9. "<u>Toilet</u> Ride"
10. "Rudolph the <u>Yellow</u>-nosed <u>Aircraft Carrier</u>"

Good Manners
1. When you receive a birthday <u>donkey</u> or a wedding <u>fish poop</u> you should always send a thank-you <u>George Washington</u>.
2. When you <u>leap</u> or burp out loud, be sure to cover your <u>butt cheek</u> and say, "I'm <u>smelly</u> sorry."

3. If you are a man and wearing a <u>diving board</u> on your head and a <u>baby throw-up</u> approaches, it's always polite to tip your <u>Scot</u>.

4. When you are at a friend's <u>hula hoop</u> for dinner, remember, it's not polite to eat with your <u>armpits</u>, take food from anyone else's <u>kneecaps</u>, or leave the table before everyone else.

5. When meeting your friend's parents, always make a <u>peeing</u> impression by greeting them <u>poopily</u>.

6. Can you tell my grandchildren are in the laugh-out-loud-at-bodily-functions stage of life? I am right there with them.

TWENTY-SIX
MORE PERKS OF PARKINSON'S

I recently treated two of my grandsons to the Pixar movie sequel, Inside Out 2, a film that brilliantly personifies emotions in a unique and entertaining way. Both this installment and the original Inside Out were particularly impactful for me as I was navigating the early stages of my Parkinson's journey when they were released.

Reminiscing about our family movie nights, when my kids were younger, we had a tradition of sharing our favorite parts of the movie and why they resonated with us. This tradition has carried on through the years, and now I have the joy of continuing it with my grandkids.

After our cinematic adventure, I eagerly asked my grandsons about their favorite moments from the movie. Interestingly, they both gravitated toward the same scenes. However, Cullen raised an eyebrow at a specific line delivered by Joy, portrayed by Amy Poehler, during a conversation with the character of Anxiety. Joy reflected, "Maybe, this is what happens when you grow up.

You feel less joy," while grappling with Anxiety's turmoil. This thought-provoking statement left Cullen pondering, and naturally, I was intrigued to hear his take on it.

Cullen's response was truly enlightening. He earnestly expressed, "Ga Ga, I don't think that is the truth." Curious, I probed further, and he elaborated, "Because you are always so joyful, so that couldn't be true. Adults can experience joy." His wise observation filled me with a rush of joy and overwhelming happiness, prompting me to discreetly wipe away tears of gratitude as I navigated us back home with some semblance of caution.

In that poignant moment, I realized that my grandchildren see beyond my Parkinson's condition; they see me for who I am and the positivity I exude. It's in those precious instances that the weight of my illness fades, and I feel truly alive and thriving. My children and grandchildren are my pillars of strength and the driving force that propels me forward. The love I share with them is the fuel that keeps me moving forward, embracing each day with renewed vigor and gratitude.

But then, the very next day, I found myself in a hospital waiting room alongside my wife and brother, anxiously awaiting news as my mother, Peggy, underwent surgery for a detached retina. To be honest, I've grown a bit wary of public gatherings as of late, especially due to my tremors. Even after over five years of living with Parkinson's, it's only my right hand and arm that experience tremors, and they tend to escalate when I feel like I'm being observed (though I know most people aren't paying attention, and those who do notice are always kind and supportive). So, I've adopted a subtle tactic of tucking my right hand into my pocket and putting on a facade of nonchalance. Just keeping it cool, folks!

Then there are those moments when I walk into a room and draw a complete blank on why I even entered. Even now, as I type this, I catch myself zoning out in front of the laptop screen, unsure if I was in the middle of writing a chapter, responding to an email, or researching for this very book! I've come to realize that these lapses aren't necessarily Parkinson's symptoms but rather signs of my aging body. I may mention my children and grandchildren often, but they truly bring me immense joy.

Another reason they bring me joy is because I love sharing the quirky mishaps that occur when I'm on my own, knowing they'll chuckle along with me. For instance, one morning after a peaceful night's sleep, I shuffled like a zombie into the bathroom to freshen up, deciding to multitask by taking a swig of mouthwash. Just as I capped the mouthwash bottle and positioned myself over the toilet, a sneeze crept up on me, leaving me utterly defenseless.

Imagine this scene: Standing before the mirror, bladder on the brink, mouth filled with mouthwash, a sneeze on the horizon...and the sheer panic on my own face. The mix of horror, absurdity, and a strong gag reflex triggered a comedic disaster! Before I could even attempt to muffle the impending explosion with my hand, the mightiest sneeze of all time erupted.

When the inevitable sneeze hit, I instinctively shut my eyes for a split second, only to reopen them and be greeted by a sight that sent me into fits of laughter. It was as if

Jackson Pollock himself had taken to my bathroom mirror as his canvas, splattering mouthwash in a chaotic yet oddly artistic display! The laughter triggered a chain reaction; my bladder protested, prompting me to plop down on the stool to contain the imminent flood caused by my uncontrollable laughter and trembling hand! After a good 20 minutes of cleanup, the room was left permeated with the invigorating scent of minty wintergreen mouthwash!

I couldn't keep this hilarious mishap to myself. There's this deep-rooted urge within me to share such moments with my wife and children because the sheer act of laughing not only boosts my dopamine levels, giving me that much-needed feel-good rush, but it also momentarily makes me forget about Parkinson's. My kids couldn't get enough of the story, while my wife simply shook her head with a chuckle. In that moment, a wave of warmth and love washed over me like never before.

My children have been my pillars of support on this Parkinson's journey. They lend a hand with physical tasks that have become challenging for me, like tending to the yard or cleaning the pool's stubborn algae. But more than the physical help, they excel at nurturing my spirit by understanding the healing power of laughter in my life. Their familiarity with my love for laughter and its therapeutic effects on my soul is a constant reminder of how cherished I am.

Not long ago, Melinda and I attended the wedding of a close friend's daughter. Like many receptions, there was a lush greenery backdrop set up for photo ops. Our daughter, Galen, was helping out as a hostess, so Melinda asked her to snap a few pictures of us. Among my children, Galen shares my quirky sense of humor the most. After capturing some still shots, she suggested a shot of Melinda and me sharing a kiss. Little did we know, she was actually recording a video, and I'm grateful she did. In the footage, I couldn't help but burst into laughter, completely unaware that my right hand was trembling throughout the whole scene.

When I pointed out my tremor to Galen, she reassured me, "Don't worry, Dad. I've got this." In no time, she had whipped up an edited version of the kissing video. The mix of laughter and Melinda's sweet peck on my cheek created a heartwarming moment, but the cherry on top? Galen had cleverly inserted a digital tambourine into my right hand, giving the illusion that I was jamming on the tambourine while getting a kiss from my wife! It doesn't get more "Parkinson's moment" than this!

Having all nine of our children, their spouses, and our grandchildren together is a rare treat, and we almost achieved this feat during a festive Christmas weekend in December 2023. If you know me, you know my love for popcorn, so it's no surprise that my children and grandchildren share the same fondness. In fact, our gift to each family member that year was a black sweatshirt emblazoned with a single word in bold white letters on the front: POPCORN!

During that memorable period, my grown children made a simple request for popcorn one evening. I decided to set the mood by placing a speaker in the kitchen and cranking up a Christmas tune composed by my kids long ago, titled "This Christmas." As the melody filled the house, our adult children kicked off an impromptu dance party, with my grandkids eagerly joining in. Before long, I found myself swaying to the beat, Melinda too, was caught up in the infectious rhythm. The air was buzzing with an indescribable joy that only a close-knit family can share. I revisit the video of that evening occasionally; it never fails to lift my spirits and bring a smile to my face.

One evening, one of my sons-in-law sprang a delightful surprise on us. He transformed our living room into a cozy movie setup, urging everyone to don their "popcorn" jerseys for a special movie night at Grandpa and Grandma's place! The film was chosen with the grandchildren in mind. Witnessing our children watch their own little ones revel in the movie brought Melinda and me immense delight, almost overwhelming us. One highlight for me was listening to our grandkids provide a lively commentary on the film, dishing out a mix of insightful critiques and wild opinions. That night, I drifted off to sleep with a heart full of contentment.

Let me squeeze in one more quick tale about my children and their delightful sense of humor before we move on to the next chapter. I promise it'll be a hoot!

The next evening, my adult children decided to host a game night and, as usual, requested some popcorn from me. Aware of their voracious appetite for our family's beloved snack, I popped not one, not two, but three massive bowls of popcorn. Little did I anticipate the surprise waiting for me in the living room. Carrying in the first bowl, I brought along a saltshaker to season the popcorn. When my daughter Glory quipped, "We prefer the salt to be stirred, not shaken," referencing my tremoring right hand, I couldn't help but chuckle. Little did I know, this was just the beginning of my children's playful antics.

Still chuckling over Glory's witty remark, I entered the room with two more brimming bowls of popcorn, only to have my son Ezra snatch my Claymore sword and declare it was time for a knighting ceremony. To add a touch of grandeur, my daughter Raina, having watched a mere five minutes of online tutorials on playing the ocarina, treated us to an impromptu fanfare as I made my entrance. This unexpected serenade sent me into another fit of laughter. Balancing a bowl in hand, Ezra kicked off the ceremony with the proclamation, "I dub thee Curator of Popcorn and Father of Many."

Just like the dancing video, I revisit the footage of the knighting ceremony every now and then, a gentle reminder of the boundless joy my family brings to my heart. I consider these moments among the many silver linings (perks) of living with Parkinson's!

TWENTY-SEVEN
AUSSIE MOMENTS 3.0

Here's a bit of history about my Aussie son-in-law, Ash. When we met, I asked him if he wanted to go look at some pawn shops with me. He thought it was a test of some sort I was putting him through. The reason? He went to my daughter, Hannah, and said in his Aussie accent, "Your dad just asked me if I wanted to go to some porn shops with him! Why would he ask me to do that?"

Hannah looked at him as only Hannah can and pronounced very slowly, "He said PAWN shop, not PORN shop." Still looking perplexed and horrified at my invitation, she spelled the word to him. "P. A. W. N." One of my favorite things about Ash is his dry sense of humor and welcoming demeanor, which makes him thinking I was asking him to visit a porn shop with me more hilarious.

During our most recent three-week stay in Australia, a prank war blossomed between my granddaughters and me. I took immense pleasure in planting plastic bugs in their beds, under pillows, and amidst their possessions each night, relishing their shrieks of terror and their vow of retaliation. The tables turned swiftly, with naked or headless Barbies finding their way into my bed, alongside the bugs, courtesy of the mischievous girls.

In a memorable retaliation, the girls orchestrated a hilarious prank by adorning my bedroom with around 15 naked Barbies striking various poses, accompanied by Krispie Kreme paper hats strewn about the room, adding an unexpected twist to the whimsical chaos.

The prank war escalated further when I unsuspectingly walked into a storm of plush fabric "snow" balls in the main living area, as Hannah armed the girls with an arsenal of snowy projectiles. Engulfed in a playful snowball battle for a good 20 minutes, Tilly and Ellie were taking no prisoners! I pled for mercy amidst the flurry of soft projectiles.

Naturally, I couldn't resist strategically placing incredibly lifelike fake cockroaches in their swimsuits, spiders on their toothbrushes, and an array of bugs nestled among the bristles of their hairbrushes. Their delightful blend of disgust and joy in being pranked fueled an escalating war that unfolded over nearly four weeks.

Their swift retaliation to my bug tactic was truly diabolical as they cleverly turned my own weapons against me. One memorable day, Ellie and Tilly orchestrated a make-believe restaurant complete with an intricate table setting and a menu predominantly featuring leftovers from a recent Thai meal. When I placed my order for green curry with chicken, the mischievous duo responded with giggles, promising to deliver my chosen dish promptly.

I could practically smell the tantalizing aroma of curry wafting through the air as they reheated it, my anticipation building for a taste of one of my favorite dishes. With great ceremony, my young servers presented me with the bowl, Ellie holding it while Tilly offered a box of salt for seasoning. As I expressed my delight at the aroma, Tilly inquired about salt, to which I agreed.

Fascinated, I reached for the salt box, only to be met with a sight that sent me into a fit of laughter mingled with a touch of revulsion. Despite ordering green curry with chicken, what lay before me was green curry with cockroaches! The meticulously arranged dish, with around ten artfully crafted cockroaches, resembled a creation worthy of Gordon Ramsay's culinary artistry.

The pièce de résistance unfolded when they conspired to apply makeup to my slumbering face. Little did they know, their mother had tipped me off to play along by pretending to doze off on the couch for a facial makeover session, setting the stage for a hilarious and unexpected twist in their prank saga.

One sunny afternoon, I made a grand announcement to the household that I intended to catch a quick nap on the living room couch, urging everyone to maintain hushed tones. The prospect of an unsuspecting canvas for their makeup artistry left the girls positively gleeful with anticipation, as I suppressed giggles while feigning slumber.

Moments later, soft whispers and the delicate sound of little feet tiptoeing around reached my ears, accompanied by the gentle rustle of the blanket ensuring I was truly asleep. The moment that almost broke my composure came when a voice, barely above a whisper, inquired right by my ear, "Are you asleep, G Pa?" I fought back the urge to burst into laughter, straining to maintain my faux slumber.

For the ensuing 20 minutes or so, I played my part as the sleeping beauty while the girls meticulously applied foundation, eye shadow, blush, and eyeliner to my face. Their eagerness led to some close calls, with brushes perilously close to my eyes. Tilly even playfully poked my face with the eyeliner brush, testing my resolve to stay "asleep" as I struggled to stifle my laughter. Their whispered commentary resembled that of a nature documentary narrator, or a golf analyst discussing a crucial putt with hushed intensity.

Once they had completed their transformation, the girls dashed off to seek validation from their mum and G Ma, eager to document their handiwork before my "awakening." I endured a few more moments of stifling laughter as they captured photos of their masterpiece, building the suspense for the grand reveal.

When the time came, the girls pounced on me, tickling and urging me to "Wake up, G Pa! See what WE did to you!"

Feigning astonishment, I inquired with mock seriousness, "What have you girls done to me?"

Their excited voices chorused, "Look in the mirror! Look!"

PARKINSON'S & RECREATION 2

Accompanied by their infectious laughter, I approached the mirror and, with feigned shock, exclaimed, "What have you girls done to me?!"

"We gotcha, G Pa! We gotcha good!" exclaimed the girls, their infectious glee dispersing even the gloomiest Parkinson's fog, banishing it into oblivion. Finally free to revel in laughter, I chuckled until my abdominal muscles ached, though, truth be told, that doesn't take much! The sound of the girls' laughter as they gleefully recounted the prank to their dad later that day, complete with photographic evidence, filled me with gratitude and a profound sense of being cherished.

Another cherished memory from our Australian adventure was the opportunity to unleash our creativity with our granddaughters. Early in the trip, Elliott handed me a notebook and pen, declaring, "These are for you, G Pa. Let's write songs together." Collaborating on a song with my granddaughter was a truly special moment. Inspired by the upcoming 5th birthday of her American cousin, Theo, we set out to craft a celebratory tune. The lyrics we penned went like this:

"Theo! Theo!
One year older makes you five years old! Theo! Theo!
One year older makes you five years old!
One year older makes you five years old!
The alpacas say, 'Happy birthday!
Happy birthday! Happy birthday, Theo!'
'Happy birthday! Happy birthday!
Happy birthday, Theo!'"

Once our song and melody were in place, we embarked on recording a video using my laptop and

GarageBand app, all set to be unveiled on Theo's special day. The joy it brought me was immeasurable, knowing the delight it would bring to them! For a front-row seat to the musical celebration, simply head to YouTube and search for Theo's 5th.

The girls' menagerie includes alpacas named Winchester and Chevalier, along with a flock of chickens that provide a steady supply of eggs. Their boundless energy and creativity meant I rarely had a dull moment; they took it upon themselves to ensure my entertainment. A standout moment of the trip was when the girls took me on a lively tour of their miniature farm, expertly narrating as I captured the adventure on video. Witnessing their vibrant personalities shine in that moment felt nothing short of heavenly—it was a slice of paradise right here on Earth, and I cherished every second of it.

One particularly unique and delightful experience I shared with the girls was creating our very own language with my granddaughter, Matilda. The spark of this linguistic innovation ignited spontaneously on our very first day there. Tilly and I dove headfirst into a conversation of complete gibberish, almost as if we were sharing the same wavelength, blurting out nonsensical phrases in perfect harmony. Responding to each other in this whimsical language felt so natural that it almost seemed like we could grasp the essence of our exchanges, at least in spirit.

Elliott would just shake her head in amusement whenever Tilly and I delved into these moments of linguistic play. I couldn't help but notice her mom, dad, and even G Ma joining in on the head-shaking fun! Tilly and I share a unique connection that transcends words; it's a bond that defies explanation but brings me immense joy. It's safe to say that this quirk isn't a symptom of Parkinson's, lol! Just another charming trait that runs in our Jernigan bloodline.

TWENTY-EIGHT
MY THURSDAY

On the morning of Thursday, May 9, 2024, en route to my massage/physical therapy session, my car decided to throw in the towel at one of Muskogee's busiest intersections during the early morning rush hour—yes, even Muskogee has its own version of rush hour. Scheduled to drop my car off at my brother's shop for a diagnostic test due to the sporadic flashing of my battery light, my plans took an unexpected detour. With the realization that my car wasn't going to budge, I activated my hazard lights and attempted to signal passing drivers to maneuver around me, which they promptly did.

It briefly felt like I was in a bustling metropolis as horns blared and voices shouted for me to clear the way. Surprisingly, the total electrical failure of my vehicle inadvertently led to a barrage of not-so-nice and colorful comments from frustrated motorists, but their words were lost on me amid the chaos. The sentiment, however, was crystal clear. As I rummaged through my wallet for my AAA card to summon roadside assistance, it dawned on me that it had vanished, prompting a call to my hero of the day, Melinda. The escalating anxiety threatened to set off my tremors in my right hand and arm as I teetered on the edge of control.

Melinda swiftly sprang into action, dialing both 911 and AAA, outlining the gravity of my predicament in the middle of a perilous traffic snarl. Assurances of immediate assistance came from both AAA and the police. After enduring several nerve-wracking minutes stranded in the middle of a four-lane thoroughfare at a major intersection, a state trooper arrived in a formidable black pickup truck, inquiring about the unfolding drama. I explained my dilemma, to which he calmly suggested, "We need to nudge you to the roadside."

My response? "There's just one tiny hiccup with that plan. I'm unable to shift gears out of park."

During the unfolding chaos, the state trooper asked if such a predicament had occurred before, to which I recounted, "Yes, it's happened before... but I think I have a solution."

Channeling my inner MacGyver, I improvised with a coffee stopper salvaged from an old Starbucks cup, locating a spot labeled "gear release" near the gearshift lever. Inserting the stopper into the designated slot magically liberated the gear shift. The trooper swiftly strategized, "We'll need to guide it leftward into the Walmart entrance."

Puzzled, I asked, "You want me to navigate across oncoming traffic?"

PARKINSON'S & RECREATION 2

His response was matter of fact, "Yes, they'll yield for us."

Over the cacophony of traffic, I hollered back at him, "I have Parkinson's and won't be able to assist much with the pushing!"

Unfazed, he reassured me, "That's fine. Just steer." Just as those words left his lips, two gallant young men pulled over, leaping out of their vehicles to lend a hand alongside the trooper in propelling my car up a gentle incline—a feat I couldn't have managed solo. It felt akin to divine intervention, sweeping away my anxiety and fear like a robust gust dispersing morning mist.

Retreating to the driver's seat, I settled in to await the tow truck's arrival. Minutes turned into an hour with no tow truck. However, in a stroke of serendipity, not one but two local police officers dropped by to check on me during this prolonged wait. The initial officer ensured my well-being and advised me to remain by the vehicle. Subsequently, the second officer inquired about my AAA membership, and upon confirmation, remarked, "It should be Morgan towing." Expressing surprise at the delay, he resolved, "They should've been here by now. Let me check if they've received the dispatch from AAA."

Following his call to the towing service, he relayed, "There's no service request on file for you in their system, so I'll have Morgan dispatch a truck and sort things out with AAA." He asked me to activate my hazard lights, and I replied, "They've been on the whole time I've been stuck." Observing their inactivity, he reassured me that the tow truck would arrive soon and inquired about my well-being. I assured him that I was alright, mentioning that my wife was waiting in her car a few lengths ahead.

Meanwhile, at the Walmart entrance, a young man at a neighboring stoplight caught my eye, waving and silently mouthing, "Need a hand? Are you okay?"

Gesturing thumbs up, I mouthed back, "I'm good. Thanks!" His kind gesture washed away the negativity hurled my way during the ordeal and soothed my soul.

After what felt like an eternity stranded in my car, a much-awaited tow truck finally rolled up, manned by a friendly young driver. Inquiring about the AAA call, I informed him that my wife had placed the call. Promptly reaching out to AAA and finding no record of the call, he deftly resolved the issue using my AAA card, promising to handle it for me.

In an unexpected yet appreciated move, he whipped out a compact battery charger and diagnostic tool, hooking it up to my battery. Managing to kickstart the car, the diagnostics revealed a dire situation—my battery and alternator were toast. Leaving the apparatus connected as a makeshift backup battery, he skillfully loaded the car onto the truck. Trying to drive to the repair shop would have been fruitless.

Touched by the young man's care, I felt compelled to express my gratitude, asking if he'd accept a tip. With a hint of reluctance, he replied, "Yes, we do accept tips," before graciously receiving the offering and delivering a simple yet profound message, "Thank you so much, sir... and God bless you."

Stepping into Melinda's vehicle, overwhelmed with gratitude for the kindness showered upon me by the

PARKINSON'S & RECREATION 2

state trooper, the helpful young men, the vigilant police officers, the kind passerby, and the benevolent tow truck driver, I felt blessed despite the anxiety and panic during the ordeal.

Divine providence seemed to have watched over me, a sentiment I was about to voice when Melinda preempted me, remarking, "It's a good thing you didn't reach the Arkansas River bridge. Imagine if you had stalled there?"

Echoing her thoughts, I acknowledged the potential disaster, given the bridge's current single-lane status due to ongoing repairs, stretching over half a mile. Reflecting on the what-ifs, I recognized the protective hand that guided me.

Clearly drained emotionally and mentally post-ordeal, I felt a profound sense of blessing and protection from the presence of the Lord and the kind souls sent my way. A newfound lightness settled deep within me, illuminating my core.

How's your day shaping up? Mine's been quite the ride. Remember, while we can't always control our circumstances, we can choose how to respond. Opting for joy has been my pick, and I recommend the same for you.

TWENTY-NINE
A CAREGIVER'S POINT OF VIEW

From Melinda:
As a caregiver, I'm Dennis's biggest fan, no doubt about it! And you know what they say, laughter is the best medicine, even when you're faced with the challenges of Parkinson's.

There are times when I feel a little discouraged, especially when I start to think about what the future might hold. But I'm a glass-half-full kind of girl. Take the other day, for instance—DJ's car decided to kick the bucket right in the middle of traffic. Talk about a headache! But after getting DJ's car towed to the repair shop and getting him home, I headed straight to Lowe's and loaded up my Ford Explorer with a mountain of mulch for the flower beds.

Now, let me paint you a picture. There I am, sweaty and exhausted, my sun hat askew, mask on to keep those pesky allergies at bay, and my glasses fogging up something fierce. I'm pulling my Explorer into the garage, determined to get this job done, when "WHAM!" I clip the right rearview mirror. Now, I know that mirror folds in as a safety feature, but in my mind,

I'm thinking, Ah, no big deal, just a little nick in the paint. Man, *was I wrong!*

I kept going, hearing this awful crinkling, scraping sound, but there was no turning back. I just had to get that car in the garage and assess the damage. When I finally got a good look, I was cringing. That mirror was hanging on for dear life! But I couldn't help but laugh. I mean, only I could manage to pull off a move like that.

It's moments like these that remind me to cherish the little joys, even during the challenges. Because let's be honest, if we can't find the humor in the chaos, what's the point? So, I'll keep on being Dennis's biggest cheerleader, laughing through the tough times, and soaking up every precious moment we have together. After all, that's what being a caregiver is all about—finding the light, even in the darkest of days.

Talk about feeling like a complete and utter fool. There I am, standing in the garage, staring at my poor, battered car, and the damage is just...ouch! The white paint and bits of wood trim embedded into the passenger door and all down the right side—it's a real mess. And that nice, crisp crinkle running all the way to the back fender? Yeah, that's not exactly the kind of "new look" I was going for.

But you know what really gets me? Despite that I feel like the world's biggest fool, Dennis is right there, asking if I'm okay. I mean, the man's already had a rough day, what with his car troubles and all, but he's still more worried about me than the state of my poor, abused vehicle. That's just the kind of man he is, you know? Always putting others first, even when he's the one who's exhausted.

And of course, when I finally muster up the courage to call him over and show him the damage, he just laughs. Yes, that's

PARKINSON'S & RECREATION 2

right: He thinks it's the funniest thing he's ever seen. "That's so you," he says, with that big, goofy grin of his while I roll my eyes at his response. I swear, sometimes I wonder if he knows me better than I know myself.

But even in the chaos, the frustration, and the sheer embarrassment of it all, there's still laughter. There's still that sense of camaraderie, that unbreakable bond that we share. And that, my friends, is what makes this journey with Parkinson's just a little bit easier to navigate.

So, yeah, I may have broken the house and my car, but at the end of the day, I've got Dennis by my side, and that's all that really matters. Now, if you'll excuse me, I've got some buffing and washing to do. Gotta make this baby shine again, you know?

Oh, I can just picture it now—me, with that signature "all in" attitude of mine, causing a little, ahem, "minor" damage to my beloved car. I mean, seriously, who else could pull off something like that?

And when our friends asked if he was upset with me, my response was, "No way!" Because I know, deep down, that Dennis could never stay mad at ME, even if I tried my best to make a mess of things.

After all, as Dennis so eloquently put it, "Cars are material things that will rust and fade away. They're replaceable, not eternal." And he's absolutely right. In the grand scheme of things, a little dent or scratch on the car is nothing compared to the unbreakable bond I and Dennis share.

Think about it: Just a few hours earlier, I was the one there for him, calling the cops, waiting with him for the tow truck, and making sure he got home safely. That's the kind of love and support we have for each other, Parkinson's or not. We're in this together, lifting each other up, fighting side by side, and finding those precious moments of joy, even on the toughest days.

I Thessalonians 5:16-18 tells us: "Rejoice always, pray continually, give thanks in all circumstances; for this is God's will for you in Christ Jesus." That's the perfect way to sum up our outlook, isn't it?

Dennis tells me, "You know you are one of a kind. And I'm so grateful to have you in my life, sharing this journey with me. So, keep on being your amazing 'all in' self, and know that I'll be right here, cheering **you** on every step of the way."

Where do I even begin? The joy that fills my heart when I get to spend time with my children and grandchildren is indescribable. Just the thought of it brings the biggest, brightest smile to my face.

You know, it's the little things that really make my day. Like when I get all dressed up, feeling fabulous, and head out with one of my daughters and my precious granddaughter for a Mother's Day tea party at a lovely, historic bed & breakfast. The crisp, floral scent of the tea, the delicate lace and china, the gentle chatter of the other guests—it all just transports me to another world filled with pure, unadulterated bliss.

And my children, bless their hearts, they really know how to make a mama feel special. The phone calls, the handwritten cards, the thoughtful gifts—it's like they've got a direct line to my heart. But you know what I treasure the most? Just being in their presence, watching them live their lives, sharing in their joys and triumphs.

Take my granddaughter, for instance. She's got this adorable habit of trying to sneak up and scare us, and sometimes, she actually pulls it off! The way her eyes light up with mischief and the sound of her giggling fills me with such unbridled delight. And then there's the times when she leaves me those beautiful wildflowers, a little surprise to brighten my day. Pure joy!

And my grandsons? With hugs, encouraging words and silly songs, they've got me wrapped around their little fingers. And don't even get me started on their card tricks and games. I may be a bit biased, but I'm pretty sure I make the best pancakes in the world, according to them, at least.

And then there's the FaceTime calls with the grandkids who live farther away. It's like a roller coaster ride! Watching them dart around, showing me their latest Lego creations or crafts is enough to make a grandma's head spin. But I wouldn't have it any other way because in those moments, I feel like I'm right there with them, sharing in their joy and wonder.

Yes, my life lived with one who struggles with Parkinson's has its challenges, but moments like those are medicine for my soul. They're the reminders that, even on the toughest days, there's always a glimmer of joy to be found, if you just know where to look. And I'm going to keep searching for it, no matter what.

I can only imagine the whirlwind of emotions you must be feeling as you navigate this journey with Parkinson's, whether you are the one who suffers or the one who cares for them. The challenges, the responsibilities, and the changes to one's everyday life are enough to make anyone feel overwhelmed at times. And yet, here I am, asking myself how to give thanks.

It's not an easy thing to do, is it? To find the gratitude, the joy, when the date nights you used to enjoy and your social connections feel like they're slipping away.

But then, you remind yourself of that powerful scripture, the one about rejoicing always, praying continually, and giving thanks in all circumstances. And that's the key. Because it's not about the circumstances themselves, it's about my God who promises to walk with us through them.

You see, the "this" that the scripture refers to isn't the burdens or the difficulties, it's the peace, the strength, the joy that God wants to pour out on us in the storm. And you know what? He's faithful. He's in control. And He's calling you—yes, you—"faithful."

I can just picture it, you know? The way the Holy Spirit fills your heart, giving you the power to rejoice, to pray, to give thanks, even when the tears are welling up and the responsibilities feel overwhelming. Because you're not in this alone. The Lord is right there with you, guiding you, strengthening you, and reminding you that your entire spirit, soul, and body belong to Him.

And that's the best news I can imagine. Because you can trust that God will give you the power, the strength, and the joy to keep pressing forward, even on the toughest days. And if you happen to break a few things or dent a few cars along the way, well, that's just part of the journey.

So, keep holding on to that truth, that promise of God's faithfulness. And know that I'm here, walking alongside you, cheering you on with my glass half full and celebrating the beautiful diamond of joy that shines even in brokenness. Because the essence of this Parkinson's journey is finding the light, even in the darkest of times.

THIRTY
STILL MORE PROOF

Reflecting on the tapestry of my life, the memories that often surface first are the ones steeped in joy. Yet, intertwined with these are experiences of great sorrow. Just as I've gleaned from my journey with Parkinson's, I've come to understand that from the depths of tragedy emerges the glimmer of hope.

Chances are the chilling echoes of the Columbine High School massacre on April 20, 1999, stir in your recollection. That fateful day saw two students unleash a horrific shooting and attempted bombing, claiming the lives of 12 students and a teacher, with 21 others sustaining gunshot wounds.

On the solemn evening of May 30, 1999, I stood at the helm of worship in Columbine, Colorado, rallying support for the victims and offering solace to the bereaved and injured. The atmosphere was laden with sorrow, a palpable weight pressing down like the burdens of the world, tangible enough to reach out and touch.

A night forever etched in memory, my heart recalls singing from the perspective of the Father, weaving words of comfort over the families, victims, and survivors of that tragic episode. Witnessing hundreds rise in need of solace, their tears mingling with the healing touch of the Holy Spirit, was nothing short of breathtaking.

I hold firm to the belief that events like the Columbine tragedy are fueled by the darkness of Satan, the deceiver, the adversary of the Almighty. Scarcely had the wounds from Columbine begun to heal when another harrowing incident shook the nation. On September 15, 1999, just four months later, a mass shooting unfolded in a place one least expected: Wedgwood Baptist Church in Fort Worth, Texas. The assailant took seven lives, wounded seven others, and took his own life.

In the wake of the tragic incident, Pastor Al Meredith rallied the congregation, declaring, "We will not give an inch to the darkness," a resolute stance that reverberated through the church. In a poignant sermon, he proclaimed, "This tragedy that the devil wanted to use to stop the people of God has ended up strengthening us," emphasizing how the adversity had united the church. Advocating forgiveness, he extended compassion to the shooter, labeling him a "poor man" swayed by evil forces. In a remarkable act of grace, Pastor Meredith and other church members even reached out to the shooter's family.

The shooting left the church sanctuary stained with blood, prompting a decision to remodel the space, erasing all traces of the horrific event. Amid this transformation, Pastor Meredith extended an invitation for me to minister to the Wedgwood community, an offer I embraced wholeheartedly.

Stepping into the auditorium, the absence of carpet and the replacement of pews with folding chairs marked the physical changes. In soundcheck, I observed individuals scattered throughout, kneeling on the floor. Initially assuming they were in prayer, I soon realized they were inscribing scriptures on the ground. When I inquired about this practice, a church staff member explained, "We're reclaiming what was taken. Turning the evil intentions into a testament of God's goodness. Those writing on the floor are replacing the bloodstains with the victorious words of God."

Led to specific spots on the floor, I was encouraged to read aloud. Near the front altar, my eyes fell upon a familiar sight, stirring emotions within me. The lyrics of one of my songs had been etched onto the floor, a poignant reminder of the power of faith and resilience in the face of darkness.

You Are My All in All
Words & Music: Dennis Jernigan
Received on: Sept. 12, 1989

Verse:
You are my strength when I am weak
You are the treasure that I seek
You are my All In All
Seeking you as a precious jewel
Lord, to give up I'd be a fool
You are my All In All

Taking my cross, my sin, my shame
Rising again! I your bless name!
You are my All In All
When I fall down You pick me up
When I am dry You fill my cup
You are my All In All

Chorus:
Jesus, Lamb of God!
Worthy is Your name!
Jesus, Lamb of God!
Worthy is Your name!

©1989 Shepherd's Heart Music, Inc.
Dennisjernigan.com • 800-877-0406
Administered by PraiseCharts.com

Guided by the church staff member, I traversed the auditorium, pausing at spots on the floor and wall adorned with verses from my songs. It was explained to me that these acts aimed to supplant painful memories with ones of hope, with my music serving as a conduit for God's love, bringing solace and healing to wounded hearts. Though soon to be concealed beneath fresh carpet and paint, the essence of truth etched in scripture and song lyrics would linger, akin to treading on sacred ground, where the victory of Jesus Christ resonated.

As recollections of past sorrows surface, amidst the looming shadows of Parkinson's, I find solace in the memory of being part of transformative events, where light pierced through the darkness, ushering in healing and love. The nights of ministry following the Wedgwood and Columbine tragedies testify to profound comfort and love.

The events of September 11, 2001, require no recounting. Four months later, on January 11, 2002, I was asked to participate in a ministry session for first responders and families of victims. Accompanied by my parents and one of my daughters, we embarked on this poignant journey.

Witnessing the tireless efforts of those sifting through the debris of Ground Zero, searching for lost loved ones, stirred a deep well of sorrow within me. In the face of such profound loss, I grappled with feelings of inadequacy, humbled by the resilience and determination of those directly impacted by the tragedy.

The ministry unfolded in the vast auditorium of a church in Greenwich Village, where I extended a heartfelt invitation for the first responders to stand as I sought to channel the Father's love through song. The sight of nearly the entire assembly rising to receive this offering of solace remains etched in my memory, a testament to the enduring power of compassion and unity in the face of adversity. Emotions ran high that night, with tears flowing freely, yet amidst the collective grief, the palpable presence of God enveloped the space, offering solace, peace, and a touch of healing to all in attendance.

It was a privilege to minister on multiple occasions at the Pentagon, extending support to service members from various military branches. In a poignant visit, I stood at the precise spot within the Pentagon where the jet had struck, alongside Lieutenant Colonel Brian Birdwell, who recounted the harrowing moment when he was engulfed in jet fuel. Both he and his wife shared how my music had been a source of strength during his arduous recovery, after sustaining severe burns over 90 percent of his body.

Reflecting on the blessings in my life, I recall with gratitude the opportunities to craft and perform theme songs for the National Day of Prayer in 2004 and 2005 in Washington, D.C. A memorable highlight was leading the national anthem at the Cannon Office Building, accompanied by the prestigious United States Marine Band.

A fervent love for basketball has been a constant in my life, despite the challenges posed by Parkinson's. While my playing style may now resemble more of an obstacle course for my grandchildren to navigate en route to the basket, the joy of the game remains undimmed. Sporting aspirations of my youth briefly flirted with the NBA dream, culminating in an invitation to minister at the 1998-99 All-Star weekend. However, fate had other plans, as the NBA lockout thwarted this potential collaboration, etching a quirky footnote in my basketball journey. The lockout, spanning from July 1, 1998, to January 20, 1999, cast a shadow over the season, resulting in a shortened 50-game schedule and the unfortunate cancellation of that season's All-Star Game.

Despite the setback, life pressed on, and my deep-rooted love for basketball paved the way for a remarkable opportunity to minister to basketball coaches at the 2005 NCAA men's Final Four in St. Louis. Accompanied by my son, we immersed ourselves in the basketball fervor, where I not only sang at the Naismith College Player of the Year Ceremony but also shared words of faith with the coaches, enveloped in the overwhelming love of God.

Finding solace in gratitude and sentimentality as the years pass, I am acutely aware of PD's threat to erode cherished memories. Motivated by this awareness, I embark on the journey of writing this book, embracing the present while looking to the future with hope and anticipation. The prospect of an eternity in the company of Jesus and departed loved ones fills me with excitement, envisioning a joyous reunion in the boundless expanse of heaven—a future brimming with endless possibilities.

"Brothers [and sisters,] I do not regard myself as having taken hold of [it yet;] but one thing [I do:] forgetting what [lies] behind and reaching forward to what [lies] ahead, I press on toward the goal for the prize of the upward call of God in Christ Jesus."

— PHILIPPIANS 3:13-14 NASB

THIRTY-ONE
THE 'F' WORD

Let me guess. When you saw and read the title of this chapter, you skipped all the other chapters and went straight to this one. Am I right?! Don't worry. I would've done the same!

As a singer/songwriter and worship leader, I was often asked to speak and sing at worship conferences around the country. One such conference was held by a group who rented the conference space at Gallaudet University in Washington, D.C., an education facility for the deaf and hard of hearing. My first thought was, "Why would an educational institution for those with hearing loss want to invite me to speak?"

My manager, with great sensitivity, explained to me, "Another group is renting the university facilities, doofus!"

I replied, "Oh. That makes sense…"

The conference was wonderful, and we heard from several amazing speakers and wonderful bands. Because we were part of the conference leadership, my band, manager, and I were given access to the green room.

On the second day of the three-day conference, I sat at a table of fellow musicians who were sharing musician jokes, like, "What does a professional drummer say when he comes to your door?" Answer; "Pizza!" Everyone loved that joke, so I went on. "How can you tell when the stage is level?" Answer: "When drool comes out of both sides of the drummer's mouth." Again, emboldened by the raucous laughter, I went on. "What do you call 3,000 accordions at the bottom of the sea?" Answer: "A great start!"

Cue the sound of crickets chirping in the awkward silence. Everyone at the table knew something I did not. Before I could escape the awkwardness, a gentleman quietly and calmly said, "I play the accordion…"

Realizing I had offended the man (as well as others at the table who obviously knew him), I blurted out, "I collect instruments of all kinds and have always wanted an accordion. I did not mean to disparage you or the accordion. Please forgive me." He, along with the rest gathered at the table, chuckled politely and went on with the meal. Literally a week after that incident, guess what I received in the mail? That kind man sent me an accordion from his own collection, and I cherish it to this day!

Drummers out there, I am sorry (not sorry) for all the drummer jokes, but I have one more that I think you will enjoy (or find mildly offensive, lol!). "Why does a drummer leave his sticks on the dashboard of his vehicle?" Answer: "So he can park in the handicapped spaces…" Yet one more indication that Parkinson's sometimes removes my filter for sensitivity...or that I'm getting old, and I don't really care what people think anymore!

While at that same worship conference at Gallaudet University, my manager at the time, Kathy, had been notified by the airline that our flight was canceled. During one of the break times, she went to the foyer of the auditorium (in the days before the prevalence of cell phones) to use a pay phone. As I write this, I wonder (as I did back then) why there was a bank of 8 or 10 pay phones at a university for the deaf. Nonetheless, the foyer was flooded with people shifting from the auditorium to various classrooms for smaller specialized sessions. Making my way to where I knew Kathy would be, I could hear her saying over the din in her loudest managerial voice, "No! F U!"

I couldn't believe my ears! Everyone at the conference knew Kathy and knew she represented me, and now she was cussing out an airline representative in such a way that everyone could hear! I jostled my way through the crowd to try and intervene, feeling as if I were in a slow-motion sequence of a horror movie while my manager continued to shout at the top of her lungs, "No! I said 'F U!'"

Now mortified, I finally reached her just as she released her final barrage of, "I said 'F U!'" At that moment, she turned to meet my gaze of horror, which silently begged the question, "What is going on? Why are you cussing out the airline? Did you know EVERYONE can hear you?!"

Ignoring me, she turned back to the phone and began reading from a sheet of paper on which she had a printout of our airline reservations. What I thought was her saying "F U" was actually her repeating the series of numbers and letters in our booking code.

She continued, "Our reservation number is '784923-FU.'" Relieved at this revelation, my anxiety disappeared, and I waited until she had completed the call to ask her what she thought people might have thought as she had yelled "F U" several times during her conversation with the airline rep. When it finally sank in, we burst into laughter that I still enjoy just as much now as I did when it happened.

The year before I was diagnosed with PD (2019), I was still accepting invitations to speak and sing at various Christian events. One of my last public appearances was for a group of Catholics at a worship conference in Ft. Lauderdale, Florida. The conference was held at a hotel that also served as our accommodations during our stay. It was at this meeting when I began to feel as if something was wrong with my voice and my mental capacity. I felt weak and as if I had to fight for every note. I had moments of brain fog, which left me confused and a bit fearful. Melinda felt I was simply fatigued and suggested I take a break and rest for a couple of hours.

After I got to our room, I felt the fog lift and felt a slight surge of energy. I assumed I had simply overextended myself and had spent too much of myself listening to the many people who stopped me during the various break times in the conference for a brief conversation.

I stripped off all my clothes to enjoy what we guys refer to as freedom. Nekkid time. Staying in a suite, I strutted around the bedroom while I put away my clothes and then headed for the living room area for a bottle of water. As I stood in the middle of the room, left hand on left naked hip, water bottle pressed firmly to my lips, the doorknob began to turn. Assuming it was Melinda (since it was mid-afternoon), I stood there proudly waiting to surprise my wife with my masculine glory.

As I stood there akimbo, in she came. It took me only a couple of seconds to realize that I did not recognize the silhouette of the woman entering the room. Only when she uttered the word, "Housekeeping!" followed by an embarrassed, "I'm so sorry, sir!" did I really understand what was taking place. As our eyes met, the look of horror on her face must have been matched by my own horrified glare. In shock, I just stood there...and then she looked down at my man parts!

Before I could even cover myself or even say, "I'm so sorry, ma'am!" she was gone. For the rest of that conference, I assumed the walk of shame—head down, eyes to the ground, hands in pockets—any time I left the room. Yep. That happened...

Now, back to the "F" word. That word is normally not in my vocabulary, but thanks to modern technology, it has made its way in— without my consent. A few years ago, someone contacted me on Facebook, inquiring about inviting me to their church for a concert. Being a supposedly tech-savvy guy, I dictated a response, saying, "You will need to talk with my booking coordinator to schedule a worship and ministry time at your church."

I received a very curt reply that read, "I can't believe you would talk to me like that!"

I read my text and discovered why I should always proofread what I've dictated before I hit the send button. It read, "You will need to talk with my f*@$ing coordinator to schedule a worship and ministry time at your church."

Surprise! I never heard from her again!

On a side note, but very much in the vein of how the "F" word has infiltrated my world, one of my grandsons, who was 5 at the time, ran to me for a hug on one of his many visits to our home. He sat on my lap and leaned toward my ear like he had something secret to tell me. I leaned in. He said in a very hushed and very serious tone, "Hey, Ga Ga. What the f#@&?"

In shock at what I thought I heard, I asked him, "What did you just say?"

He repeated himself while I tried to control the urge to burst out laughing, "What the f#@&?"

I said, "Son, that is not an appropriate word for you to say." His oldest brother, who had been listening from the piano bench where he had been noodling out a quiet tune, calmly replied, "He heard that at school."

Still trying to keep from laughing, I said to him, "It doesn't matter if other people are saying it or not. There are better words to use than that word. Would you try and use a different word next time you think of saying it?"

He nodded, saying, "Yes, sir," and was off playing with the other kids while I finally had a release of laughter...and immediately looked for another adult to tell what had just happened!

In April 2023, our son, Ezra, who works in sound design and deals with popular and prominent artists and bands, was at a bar listening to a set by Copeland as a part of his job. When he went to pay his bar tab, the bartender noticed his last name and asked if he was related to Dennis Jernigan. Ezra replied, "Yes. He's my dad."

The bartender replied with great passion, "Your dad's a f*@$ing great singer! I heard him several times at my church when I was young...and my parents love his music." Ezra got a big kick out of the bartender's response and thought I would enjoy hearing it. Is it wrong that I kind of appreciated the man's passionate and colorful response?

THIRTY-TWO
SEEN, UNDERSTOOD, AND DEEPLY LOVED

While dropping Cullen off at the Kay house after our regular Thursday afternoon time together, Ronald was outside playing in the front yard and had a Mandalorian helmet on. He ran up to me and gave me a great big hug, and I said, "This is the way," to which he replied without missing a beat, "This is the way." I felt so absolutely loved in that moment...and then he melted my heart when he said, "Ga Ga. I am praying for you to get better from Parkinson's." I honestly felt a tinge of regression of the disease rather than aggression for the next few minutes and beyond. Clarity of mind. A sense of peace. An obvious cessation of my tremor. I know that sounds crazy, but I DO have Parkinson's so I understand how you could think I'm losing it. However, that feeling of the constant and intense battle with Parkinson's markedly subsided even if for a few hours. Priceless.

While waiting at the barn for my son Ezra's dog, June, to come in for the night, Cullen and I listened to an announcement on ABC News concerning Parkinson's disease via an Instagram post. The announcement was exciting and encouraging but proved to be a very poignant moment between Cullen and me. The announcement basically said (I'm paraphrasing), "It was announced today (April 14, 2023) that the Michael J. Fox Foundation for Parkinson's Research had recently discovered a biomarker, a misfolded protein, that may be able to determine if a person has PD, which, in turn, may eventually lead to better treatments for those who have PD."

We watched and listened intently, and I could tell he was very encouraged by the good news being announced and by the joyful excitement in the reporter's delivery of that announcement. But right in the middle of the news report, I was shocked back into the reality of my circumstance when the reporter said, "Right now, of course, there is no cure." My hope was that Cullen had missed that brief statement and that I had not given away any semblance of fear or dismay that might frighten him. I could tell instantly that he had heard every word, but my heart was overwhelmed when, immediately after that passing statement, Cullen leaned into my shoulder and put his arm around me and just held me quietly as we listened to the rest of the report. I don't know how to adequately describe how I felt except to say, seen, understood, and deeply loved by my grandson.

On that same evening, Cullen, Ronald, Harold, and Zella were staying with us while their parents had a date night. Around 8:30 p.m., they asked if I would read another chapter from *The Puzzle*. It happened to be chapter 3, which is titled "Cullen's Surprise." Spoiler alert: Details about some heavy plot points are about to be revealed.

It is in this chapter that Cullen, on his way to Bren, is met by a friend who died several years ago: His mom's horse, Wendy. Of course, Cullen is shocked, delighted and confused all at the same time and weepingly asks Wendy this question:

"Why did you have to die? Why does anyone or anything have to die?"

"I do not fully understand yet myself," replied Wendy, honestly, "but I do know life and death go hand in hand and that you cannot have one without the other. And I can promise you this, Cullen. In the end—in the grand scheme of all that is earth and Bren—life ALWAYS wins!"

As I read that statement in the darkness of the music room where the children had made pallets on the floor because they were getting sleepy, I suddenly found myself surrounded by all four of the children wrapping their arms around me in the most precious bear hug. It was difficult to keep reading without getting overly emotional. It is simply amazing to me the capacity of our grandchildren to sense the emotional needs of others and to respond with compassion.

After I finished reading the chapter, the children laid back down and five-year-old Zella sang this to me and slayed my heart:

"*You are my Ga Ga*

My only Ga Ga
You make me happy
When skies are grey
You'll never know, dear
How much I love you
Please don't take my Ga Ga away"

I was speechless.

A few days later I received this text from Zella's mom: "Last night Zella stated, 'Going to bed is the worst!' and promptly started crying, LOL! I wish you could hear how she said it, haha! So dramatic!"

I live my life moment by moment, from laughter to tears and back to laughter again. Parkinson's just makes me realize the value of living in the moment, and God uses my grandchildren to remind me to live my life in that way.

THIRTY-THREE
HOW I THINK

"Every man dies. Not every man really lives."

— WILLIAm WALLACE, *BRAVEHEART*

I want to be able, at the end of my life, to look back and say what a wonderful journey it was despite all the ups and downs, twists and turns, pains and sorrows, and have no regrets. Even though I have Parkinson's, I plan to live and die well.

This chapter is just a slathering of random thoughts that don't necessarily have anything to do with Parkinson's per se but will give insight into the occasional eccentricities and the sometimes quirkiness of my way of thinking.

After sharing a chapter from my first book on Parkinson's with my Patreon members, I received the following message: "Have not had a PD diagnosis but do get tremors quite frequently. I laugh them off, but it makes keeping food on your fork very difficult at times. :-)

Thank you, Dennis, for being so transparent and sharing your journey with us all. I now call it…Shaky Fork Syndrome."

Proof that I am either a person with ADHD or a nerd (or, perhaps, both), my mind just changes thought in mid-stream like a dog seeing a squirrel and taking off in an entirely new direction.

Some neat trivia for you. Two famous sayings that almost everyone is familiar with were written by J.R.R. Tolkien in *The Fellowship of the Ring*. "All that is gold does not glitter" and "Not all those who wander are lost" are the beginning lines of a poem about Aragorn known as "The Riddle of Strider," quoted by Gandalf in his letter to Frodo in Book I, Chapter 10, and offered as a means for the hobbit to determine whether Strider is indeed Aragorn. Just thought you guys might enjoy some of the weird things I think about.

A Grab Bag of Too Much Information

My Aussie son-in-law, Ash, sent me a picture of a product sold in Australia called Camel Balls, a type of sour bubble gum. The picture reveals the hind quarters of a cartoon male camel with his very large testicles hanging in a very large scrotum.

He said, "This one's for you, Denis."

I responded, "That's nuts…and scrotally awesome!"

He wrote back, "Haha … I knew you would find it hilarious!"

I added, "It was the perfect thing to see just before I hit the 'sack' tonight, lol! It is also appropriate the way you misspelled my name, lol!" Of course, I was referring to the way he spelled Dennis as Denis...which is one letter away from penis. Parkinson's allows me to occasionally engage with my 13-year-old mind!

Other uses for Parkinson's: Professional Etch-a-Sketch Shaker and Bartender
Each year, my son Ezra and I go to the local Renaissance Fair. This year, watching the jugglers while suffering with Parkinson's was trippy like I imagine an LSD trip might be. After watching for only a few seconds, I had to find a shady place to sit down!

Then, while I was climbing the bleachers at the falconry show, a woman almost my age reached her hand to help steady me as I walked up the bleachers. It felt like a disaster waiting to happen in very slow motion...like the crippled leading the crippled!

I told Ezra that I get nervous about people seeing me shake when we're in public. He asked, "Would it help if I did a dance routine? I love you!"

I don't know why I just thought about this, so chalk it up to serendipity or senility. Take your pick! When I was walking around the James Robison Bible Conference, circa 1986, in the Ft. Worth Arena, holding our daughter Annē and wearing a flannel shirt and jeans with suspenders (it was a look) and Jeanne Rogers wanted to introduce me to the 15,000 people gathered there, I was, at once, mortified!

She called out for me to stand so I raised my hand and shouted, "I'm over here, Jeanne!"

She seemed horrified. How do I know this? When she saw me, she said, "You're wearing suspenders! I wanted to introduce you and you're wearing suspenders?!" I put Annē down and unclipped the suspenders so fast it sent them flying over my shoulders like two bungee cords being simultaneously released, coming to rest behind me and out of sight. The entire place went wild with laughter because my response had been broadcast on the two mega screens on either side of the main stage.

At a recent church gathering, another lady asked for prayer because she was having a difficult time sleeping and short-term memory lapses. One of the men jokingly suggested she use a memory foam pillow. I said, "I use a memory foam pillow, and it seems to have no effect on my ability to remember things! Maybe I need to get a bigger pillow!"

Random convo from our WhatsApp Family Chat
Galen: Can I use cookie dough that's been in the fridge for two days?
Me: Yes. You can always use it to throw at people in small round clumps.

Dad jokes: When Israel recently broke his toe, I wrote, "That's 'toe' bad, son. You need to 'toe' the line and be more careful. I 'toe-tally' understand. Don't say I 'toed' you so. Have some 'toe-fu' for lunch for comfort. Did you need to call for a 'toe' truck? It's going to be a good day 'toeday' anyway. I think you need to be tested for 'TOEV-ID.'"

Random Dumb Dad/Man Things
The time I set up a skateboard ramp next to the deep end of the pool and encouraged the boys to ride their

PARKINSON'S & RECREATION 2

bikes down the hill next to the pool, hit the ramp, and splash down in the pool comes readily to mind in this category. I then encouraged my boys to try and ride the bikes underwater from the deep end to the shallow end. I gave the all-too-familiar warning, "Don't tell your mother." Our secret was safe until the day Melinda noticed tread marks on the bottom of the pool.

Parkinson's Does Not Win When You Have a Chainsaw!

That was the headline I sent my family while working on chopping down a tree in our back yard that died over the winter. I sent my family a picture of the work I had done along with the caption, "Parkinson's does not win when you have a chainsaw!" I also, of course, posted it on YouTube.

After the chainsaw post on my YouTube channel, I received the following email from a friend in Florida:

> "Dennis,
>
> Was glad to see your new post. Thought this response should be between me and you instead of YouTube. You know I own and manage a lawn care and landscaping company so I would gladly fly up to OK and use your chainsaw and do it for you so...you better not hurt yourself. I expect to see two more Parkinson's Moments episodes regarding this event, if not... you better be really hurt, really, really hurt because I would also fly to hurt you for doing that to yourself. Love you, Dennis! Be safe."

My response:

"Haha, thanks! That made me laugh, brother. I am actually taking some wise counsel this week and taking time to replenish my soul and not worry about getting so much done. I'm still going after the tree, by golly, lol!

Love you, Chad/Dennis Jernigan's Personal OSHA Rep."

My friend sent me the following email with a faux OSHA Rep. card:

Chad
DENNIS JERNIGAN'S PERSONAL OSHA REP
321-4Safety (472-3839)
4Safety.com
Keeping the customer and community safe and secure from the attitude of, "Hey, watch this!"

I replied:

My alternative to OSHA? OGDAD: Old Guy's Dumb and Dangerous Deeds

Random thought: I can tell my tremor is progressing, or maybe it's just that I am tired in the evening after a long day's work, when I am playing solitaire on my phone. My right index finger tremors constantly at times and seems to have a mind of its own. My brain sends a thought to my finger to shuffle through the deck three cards at a time, but my finger has other ideas and moves so rapidly that I've shuffled through six, nine, or 12 cards before I even know what has happened!

More Parkinson's Moments

One Saturday at the local Renaissance Fair, Ezra and I had our traditional turkey leg and walked around the grounds just enjoying being together. He makes me laugh so much. We went straight from there to the movie theater to watch Guardians of the Galaxy 3. Melinda and I had seen it two nights before on our date night and I wanted to see it with my son because he's fun to watch movies with and because I missed so much banter and dialog from laughing the first time through.

Near the end of the movie, I needed to go to the bathroom so badly, but I didn't want to miss much, even though I had already seen it once, so I ran from the theater to the bathroom and did my business, then ran back into the darkened theater and sat down in my seat. As I looked to each side of me, I did not recognize either person as my son. I am sure the people thought they had just had their private space invaded by a stalker. In fact, the fear and dread on their faces said as much. I then felt a tap on my shoulder from the row behind. It was Ezra saying, "Dad. That's not your seat. You missed it by one row." A true Parkinson's moment.

Holding my four-month-old granddaughter Winifred and having one of my daughters remind me to not shake the baby too much because of my tremor…to avoid shaken baby syndrome. Too sketchy?

Several of the grandchildren once asked me to let them play some of the instruments in my collection. I picked up my violin that I have not played in over 35 years. I discovered that I now have the ability to play a perfect tremolo and very rapid Pizzicato notes due to the tremor in my right hand, lol!

My friend, Kathy, is an awesome comedienne. After watching a comedy special, I emailed her and asked, "Have you seen Leanne Morgan's comedy special on Netflix called 'I'm Every Woman'? If not, I think it would be worth your time. You're welcome."

She replied, "Yes I have! I like her! Kathleen Madigan is a fave of mine and [another friend] says she has my cadence."

My response, "I'll check her out. That sounds different than I meant it to. Uh oh! I hear the PC popo sirens now! Gotta go!"

She sent back a slew of laughing-with-tears emojis and three fire emojis.

Parkinson's has not robbed me of my ability to laugh and find humor in the simple things.

Our daughter Annē's iPhone's camera was shaking because it was dying and I said, "It must have Parkinson's. I guess it's contagious."

Our son Israel, concerning my incessant dad jokes and PD, asked: "When does the silence part kick in?"

Need I say more?

THIRTY-FOUR
MELINDA-ISMS

"I cannot leave a utensil or a glass on the kitchen counter for even 30 seconds without it disappearing into the dishwasher."

— DENNIS JERNIGAN

My wife, Melinda, is absolutely the most amazing person I know. No one makes me feel like I can do anything like she does. No one is as decisive when it comes to a plan of action. No one is better at do-it-yourself projects. No one is more beautiful than her. No one sings better than her. No one is better at problem-solving than her to me. No one is smarter than her. She is simply amazing, and she keeps me laughing like nobody else at the same time! Here are a few examples:

While watching Transporter 3, Melinda thought the female lead looked like the girlfriend of a character from another movie. She said it was a spy movie with lots of action just like the movie we were watching. She kept trying to give me clues but her clues made no sense to me. She remembered there being a lot of car chases and a lot of fighting, just like in Transporter. She said the main guy is a buddy of George Clooney. I thought of Ocean's Eleven and asked, "Do you mean Brad Pitt?"

She said, "No. I believe the movie was called John Damon."

I replied, "I've never heard of a movie called John Damon. Do you mean Matt Damon and The Bourne Identity? She snorted loudly as she burst into uncontrollable laughter, and we giggled for several minutes.

Three years ago in Fort Lauderdale, a man named Chad wanted to get to know me and asked if I could join him for coffee after my ministry time. Due to circumstances beyond his control, namely a hurricane and a dying cat, we could not keep our coffee date. He seemed so disappointed. I told him we could keep in touch and that I would give him my personal phone number but that he could not share it with anyone else because, if he ever did, Melinda would cut his balls off! My go-to answer when people ask for my number…because she has said it so often. Melinda means business!

While Melinda was filling out a check on her birthday, October 16, she asked me, "What is today's date?" And we laughed—a lot!

After watching one of our favorite TV shows, Melinda and I lowered our recliners at the exact same time and

PARKINSON'S & RECREATION 2

stood at the exact same time...and we both noticed. I said, "We should put together a synchronized recliner routine."

We got so tickled Melinda buckled over and said, "Stop! You're gonna make me pee my pants!"

In December 2023, we were watching a spy series while Melinda worked on her jewelry in her chair next to mine. At one point she asked, "What did he just do?"

I said, "You've got to watch. I can't explain every scene to you."

Her response? A perfect Melinda-ism. "It's hard to watch when I'm not watching!"

Once, when I went to give her a good morning kiss, instead of saying "Good morning," she said, "Goodnight." Once again, we could not stop laughing.

I answered, "It seems like you want me to go to bed a bit early today," and we laughed some more. Of course, that evening at bedtime, I leaned over to give her a kiss and said, "Good morning."

Our son, Ezra, enjoys bowling and is involved in several leagues. Many years ago, someone had given me my own bowling ball complete with my name etched in the ball. Since Parkinson's does not lend itself to bowling, I gave the ball to Ezra. At that point in his bowling career, he had three balls used for three reasons, depending on the lanes he was using. Melinda asked him to show her his balls. I sat there anticipating what was to follow. I was not disappointed. "I enjoy seeing your balls," was Melinda's reply to Ezra in regard to his bowling balls. This comment was made at a family gathering in March 2024 and was wonderfully awkward!

Ezra showed his mom a new beer brewed in OKC, an IPA. Melinda tasted it and said, "It tastes lemony. Is it a shandy?"

Glory said, "According to the label, it is definitely not a shandy." Then she caught my eye, and we got tickled. Mom then said, "It doesn't taste too beery. I don't like it when beer tastes too beery." I had to leave the table.

On February 9, 2019, my 60th birthday, Melinda was asking me to help her with something she was working on and said, "Hold this but don't touch it!" What would you have done?

On April 14, 2024, Melinda was making cookies for some of our children and grandchildren. She put the leftovers in freezer bags and instructed one of our daughters to put them in the freezer. Our daughter asked, "Why?"
Melinda answered, "I put them right in the freezer because I like them gooey. Because I do not like them to get hard." Which is it? Frozen solid or gooey are OK. Hard. Not so much...

On November 6, 2020, Melinda was talking with one of the children about one of their friends trying to decide what to name their newborn son. Melinda asked what names they were considering. Our daughter simply replied, "Harley."

Melinda didn't miss a beat. "Don't name him Harley because he didn't have any teeth." Of course, Melinda was referring to a distant relative of hers who did not have his teeth in adulthood...and just how were we supposed to know that?

I told Melinda my tremors were mostly triggered by anxiety, and she said, "That's because it affects your mind and that's psychological."

"Thank you, Captain Obvious," I replied.

One afternoon, Melinda complained she looked like a homeless person with her pants becoming worn out and then realized she had her shirt on inside out.

In March 2023, I was praying at bedtime for Melinda and kissing her goodnight when my glasses fell off and slammed into her nose and mouth!

Melinda was trying to think of the new Marvel TV series so we could watch the next episode. I asked, "What's the name of the show?"

She said, "You know. The show with Iron Flask."

"Who is the Iron Flask?" I asked.

She kept saying, "You know! We've watched it before! The show with Iron Flask!" After a few seconds it dawned on me what she was trying to say. I asked her if she meant the show about Nick Fury called Secret Invasion.

She said, "Yes!"

I burst into convulsive laughter and screamed, "You said 'Iron Flask'! There is no character by that name ANYWHERE on TV!"

She began to laugh, saying, "But you know what I meant!"

"Nobody could have known what you meant!" I replied.

I woke up and smelled an amazing aroma from something Melinda was cooking. I went into the kitchen and asked her what she was making, and she said, "Remember, I'm making what I told you I would make you yesterday."

I asked what she meant, and she said, "You know… You know…"

"Know what?" I asked.

"You know I told you I would make you…pop tarts!" she said. At that moment, I remembered she had told me she was going to make me a calzone.

"Do you mean 'calzone?'" Much laughter ensued.

While watching one of our favorite shows, The Good Doctor, Melinda said, "If I didn't have to deal with people, I would've been a doctor."

We were watching America's Got Talent in June 2023 when Ahren Belisle came on. He suffers with cerebral palsy, which has rendered him unable to speak. Yet he is a standup comedian and uses a text-to-speech app, which makes his "voice" sound like Stephen Hawking. He was

PARKINSON'S & RECREATION 2

amazing and very funny. At one point, he made a joke about how he thought he could beat Stephen Hawking in a race but that, if the race was downhill, then he would be screwed. He did an amazing job and afterward Melinda said, "I hope Stephen Hawking saw him."
I replied, "Stephen Hawking is dead."
Mom said, "I guess I don't know much about Stephen Hawking." Of course, we snorted with laughter and got the giggles once again.

Some of the funniest things happen as we grow older. Things that might have embarrassed us before cease to do so, lol! Like the day Melinda came to me at the end of the day and said, "My bra has felt weird all day long. And guess what? I realized I had put it on backwards!"
All I said, amidst uncontrollable laughter was, "Let me write that down!"

While I was having a foggy day, Melinda asked me to go to Lowe's with her to pick up 18 bags of mulch. Yeah...she likes to mulch things. She wanted to split a burger and fries at a local ice cream shop, so we did. I felt and thought I was absolutely useless to her. She felt we had spent quality time together. After we got home, she said, "Thanks for going with me. It was really fun!"
I dryly answered, "We picked up mulch..."
"Yeah," she said, "and it was really fun. I just like being with you."
I lifted my hands and made less-than-excited jazz hands and softly said, "Yay?" We got tickled and just called it a day.

I asked Melinda if she wanted raspberry jelly for her biscuit from KFC. She responded with, "No I just want hutter and bunny." She meant to say, "butter and honey."

Here's an email exchange between Melinda and me after she scraped the side of her car against the garage door:

Melinda: "So I just got my car in and got out and assed the damage."

Me: "I am sitting here working on your chapter when I came across this phrase in your email. My question: How did you ass the damage?" (Of course, she meant to say "assess!")

Nobody makes me laugh more than Melinda and I do not laugh at her expense. I laugh because she brings me so much joy and gives me the freedom to laugh when I need to laugh and to cry when I need to cry. She is simply amazing. If you want to know the real Melinda, read the following paragraph:

After listening to the Dennis Jernigan Podcast episode about the song "The Broken Part of Me," Melinda called me weeping and telling me how angry she was at me for not warning her about the song. In reality, though, she was calling to say how angry she was at Parkinson's for what it was doing to me and to our family. She told me she did not see me as broken at all but as the man she married almost 40 years ago. Her anger made me feel like she was fighting for me, and it did something deep in my soul. It made me want to fight all the more against the disease, against its progression, and against any hold it has upon my life.

The Broken Part of Me
Words & Music: Dennis Jernigan
Received on: April 23, 2015

Verse
I have seen my share of pain
I have known deep sorrow
I've walked the desert void of rain
Felt no hope for tomorrow
I am broken
My heart undone
I am broken
I come

Chorus
Take the very heart of me!
The broken part of me
And put it back together!
Put me back together!
Take the broken heart of me!
The broken part of me
And put it back together!
Put me back together in You!
Only in You!

Verse
My heart is a storm-tossed wreck
Hopeless, wounded, drifting

DENNIS JERNIGAN

In need of Solid Rock to stand on
When the sands are shifting
I am broken
My heart undone
I am broken
I come

Repeat Chorus

©2015 Shepherd's Heart Music, Inc.
Dennisjernigan.com • 800-877-0406
Administered by PraiseCharts.com

THIRTY-FIVE
G PA SPEAKS OWL!

Grandkids are like caffeine for my soul. They give me a charge and make me feel good even if I am having a foggy Parkinson's day. Thank you for bearing with me as I share a few more of their life-giving moments:

Theo asked what type of houses clowns have. Now I cannot stop thinking about and wondering that myself!

Before they could even read, I taught the grandkids to say John Deere whenever I pointed to the name on the Gator steering wheel. All I have to do is point to the name and ask them what it spells and they respond instantly with, "John Deere!"

We have a toy wooden barn built by my dad for my children. It is such a special blessing, endearing and hilarious, to see my children's children now playing with that barn. Theo calls the little guy in the play barn "Shaun Deer" instead of John Deere.

In late July 2023, Edison and Theo were playing rock, paper, scissors on the way to Muskogee. Edison, then 2 ½, made an addition to the game: He introduced a cutting board and cheese.

Kay Kids' 2024 New Year's *Resolutions*
Ron: "Mom, what are your New Year's resolutions?"
Annē: "Well, I think I would like to be a better mom. Maybe not yelling as much and saying, 'I love you more.'"
Ron: "You don't need to change anything. You're perfect the way you are! You're the best mom! You don't need to change."
Annē: "Oh, thanks buddy. What are your resolutions?"
Ron: "I want to try a new flavor of ice cream from Braums!"
Annē: "Ok. What flavor are you thinking?"
Ron: "Gingerbread!"
Annē: "Ok. I think I could get some tomorrow. What else?"
Ron: "I want to teach Rocky (a dog) to roll over. And I also want to do that wolf painting you got me."
Annē: "Ok, I think those are good resolutions!"
Ron: "Ok!"
And that ended the conversation. LOL

Cullen's Resolutions
"Try a new exotic food."
"Like what?" Annē asked.

PARKINSON'S & RECREATION 2

"I don't know! And to make a cherry pie! Um, and I have one more. I'm gonna learn how to build a house... well a bird house."

"Anything else?"

"Nope. But one of my other resolutions is to stay up all night!"

Ronald: "I've been holding in all my farts today, so I've really got to fart."

Theodore changed the title of my song, "You Are My All In All" to "Hot Cheesy Cheetos!"

Hannah: "Dad, Matilda constantly asks me if you're able to do certain things. Yesterday she asked if you get to NOT drive slow in a school zone because you have Parkinson's. Like it gives you a free pass to not follow rules."

My first thought? She thinks like I think. And, yes, I think Parkinson's gives me a free pass to not follow rules.

I love to laugh, and my grandkids make me laugh a lot. So I'd love to share more of what makes me laugh with you.

Matilda says "piñana," not "piñata."

More Edisonisms: Bluhsanga = lasagna. Blandaid = bandaid.

Theodore said, "I keep having dreams that in heaven, God made the earth a big fruit and you can eat it." Then he said he keeps having dreams that he's in heaven. In his dreams, the earth is made of an orange.

Zella, speaking to her mom as they drove by a cemetery, said, "Graves always make me think of Grandma Zella." When her mom asked why, Zella replied, "It's because I miss her and have never met her because she's dead."

From daughter Raina: "Theo had a hard time in the car this morning and 'I Am a Sheep' came on and he immediately calmed down then asked to play it again twice more. He said, 'Sheep and shepherds help me calm down.'"

Raina: "Edison escaped out of one of our buildings at church today and ran into the road and started to try to pull his pants down by the grass. When ya gotta go, ya gotta go!"

Annē: "Cullen just said something very profound. If you were to put a Google camera on trash trucks, you would get updated Google map photos every week."

Edison, who calls mosquitos "skamitos," said at age 3, "I want to be a dad so I can get mail."

Five-year-old Theodore asked, "What do clouds taste like? I bet they taste like nothing. I wouldn't eat a rain cloud. I want to eat thunder."

PARKINSON'S & RECREATION 2

Raina: "We were at a stoplight and Edison yells, 'Look! A primary color car!' It was yellow."

Our 8-year-old grandson, Harold, also has a keen eye for explaining life. Case in point: "If worms die in the ground, then it's perfect 'cause they are already buried."

Seven-year-old Matilda is so proud to be my granddaughter and that touches my heart in a very comforting, healing way. Her mom, Hannah (the Aussies) sent me the following: "Matilda is taking dad's Parkinson's book to her 'family history' day tomorrow. She had to write a sentence about her family history and wrote (copied) the biography on the back of the book, lol! She is so proud."

Hobbies vs. Jobs

After taking me on a FaceTime tour of her parents' home office workstations, Mia asked me what I did for a job. I told her I wrote songs and books. She said, "Those sound more like hobbies than jobs."

Grandma tells Mia, "Well, you know your grandpa is famous, right?" Mia's response. "Yes, like Barbie?"

Mark, after reading the book, *The Puzzle*, sent me the following text when I asked him what he thought of it: "It was amazing (smiling starry-eyed emoji). It was sad (frowning teardrop emoji) and it was joyful (smiling emoji). Thanks for the book (pile of books emoji)."

While Ezra was playing a melancholy tune at the piano, Zella walked up to him and said, "A lot of people have died in this world. Is that why you're playing this song?"

Raina: "Theo argues with me all the time that 'You Are My All In All' isn't Grandpa's song." (It's my all-time most sung, most heard song.)

Raina: "Edison (at age 2) got in the back of the car as we were loading everyone up, and I said, 'Get back in your seat.' He says, 'No,' then I say, 'What would happen if we got in a wreck, and you were back there?!' Edison's response? 'Arrest me!'"

From my daughter, Annē, another conversation with Zella: "While we were driving, I pointed out a VW beetle and told her that was a bug.
   Since she was sitting in the back, she said, "You can punch me when we get home if you want."

We have a lot of owls in the woods around our home. Almost every night around dusk, I go outside and try to make the sound of a barred owl. Of course, I make a video of me trying to sound like an owl in the hopes of capturing a response from somewhere deep in the woods. Often, an owl responds. On a recent evening, I was able to capture my feeble attempt at calling a barred owl and, much to my glee, I recorded the very unmistakable call of a barred owl responding to me. I immediately sent the video to all my grandchildren and got the following response from my Aussie family:

PARKINSON'S & RECREATION 2

Hannah: "I should have gotten the girls' reactions! They were SO impressed!"

Elliott said, "G Pa speaks owl!"

While out on a recent afternoon walk with her children, Raina remarked to them, "We are in the neighborhood."

Edison replied, "We are NOT in the neighborhood!"

"Then where are we?" Raina asked.

Edison: "We are in Mexico."

Annabell said to her mom recently, "You are being really nice today. You must be in a good mood."

THIRTY-SIX
PLANNING AHEAD

"A man who has not prepared his children for his own death has failed as a father."

- KING T'CHAKA OF WAKANDA TO HIS SON, T'CHALLA (*BLACK PANTHER*)

On a recent Wednesday evening, we were livestreaming our worship gathering in the cozy confines of our living room at All In All Church. As the final notes of worship faded away, I stepped closer to the camera to offer a heartfelt prayer for all our viewers before bidding them farewell. However, as I fumbled to end the session, I found myself at a loss without my glasses. With a chuckle, I apologized to our online audience, requesting their patience as I searched for my missing spectacles. Just then, a chorus of voices from our church family chimed in, pointing out, "They're on your head!"

I couldn't help but jest, attributing the oversight to either a "Parkinson's moment" or a "Senior moment" or a mix of both!

With each passing year, I've come to anticipate such comical mishaps. Embracing the natural progression of aging, I find solace in the realization that growing old need not be a daunting prospect but rather a journey to be embraced with joy. This very sentiment served as a driving force behind the creation of this book.

Maintaining a cheerful outlook has been key, and part of that involves planning ahead for the golden years. Uncertain of what tomorrow may bring, I've chosen to cast worries aside. My wife, Melinda, and I have taken proactive steps to ensure that our children and grandchildren need not fret about our well-being. By establishing a living trust and appointing one of our children as power of attorney, we've sought to lift the burden of financial concerns, funeral arrangements, and end-of-life decisions from their shoulders. With signed Do Not Resuscitate orders in place, we've made it clear that we wish to gracefully transition to the next chapter when the time comes to return home to the Lord. By openly communicating our desires, we aim to pave the way for a future free of uncertainties, grounded in thoughtful preparation.

As I write these words, I find myself immersed in the thoughtful planning of my own memorial service. My aim is not to center it around myself but rather to impart blessings upon my children and grandchildren, urging them to embrace life without the shackles of regret, fear, or worry. The blueprint for my memorial service is elegantly simple—a selection of cherished songs to be sung, passages of scripture to be shared, and heartfelt declarations of love for each of my dear descendants. They, above all else, are my true legacy. Not my music, not my writings, not my achievements, but the love and wisdom I pass down to them. I yearn for them to celebrate my life rather than mourn my departure, embarking on their own adventures guided by unwavering faith and boundless joy in the Lord Jesus Christ.

When I was just 14 years old, the loss of my beloved grandmother Jernigan left an indelible mark on my heart. Our bond ran so deep that amid organizing her memorial service with her pastor, I took it upon myself to gather all the materials she had meticulously prepared for the occasion. Her foresight included specific scripture passages for each grandchild and my parents, along with songs meant not for her pleasure, but as beacons of encouragement for us. Among them, she had chosen "I Want to Stroll Over Heaven With You" as my personal anthem.

This poignant gesture has been a guiding light for me, reassuring me that our reunion is but a heartbeat away. The day I walked into the room where my grandmother's pastor and my father were immersed in funeral arrangements, I calmly placed the stack of her instructions and songbooks on the table before them. With a simple declaration—"Here are Grandma Jernigan's wishes for her funeral. Everything you need is in this stack"—I left them speechless, secure in the knowledge that her love had entrusted me with the sacred task of honoring her legacy. As I departed, grief mingled with unwavering faith, for I knew in my heart that our bond transcended earthly bounds, paving the way for a joyous reunion in the arms of our Savior.

I don't lose sleep over my children, even though we may not always see eye to eye on politics or spirituality. What truly matters is our unwavering love for each other, a bond that brings me profound peace. As Melinda and I like to say, if God has seen us through, He can surely do the same for our children. So why fret? Our offspring are cut from a different cloth; they possess resilient spirits, nurtured by our teachings to embrace boldness, courage, and a victorious mindset. Their life choices are theirs to make, and we trust them to navigate their paths with grace and strength. My personal mantra, come what may, remains refreshingly simple: Amid life's storms, I fix my gaze upon Jesus. He is my beacon of hope, my source of strength, and my eternal joy.

Discussing end-of-life matters with our children led to a lighthearted yet heartfelt moment years ago when one of my sons quipped, "Dad, if it's up to me, you're heading to the 'home' ASAP!"—referring to a retirement residence. The jest, accompanied by a laugh, struck a chord in my heart, a testament to the deep love and trust we share. It's moments like these that underscore the depth of our familial bonds and the safety our children feel in expressing themselves freely. Melinda and I are on the brink of another significant decision, determining the fate of our earthly remains once we've departed. Our inclination leans toward securing a single cemetery plot, where our ashes will rest side by side. But why opt for a plot at all?

For us, cemeteries are sacred grounds of remembrance, where stories of generations past are woven into the fabric of memory. They serve as gathering spots for older and younger kinfolk to honor our departed loved ones, especially on poignant occasions like Memorial Day. My mother's tradition of convening our family at the cemetery each year for heartfelt reflections on those who've journeyed into eternity fills me with a sense of peace and gratitude for the legacy that paved the way for my existence.

In the grand scheme of things, it all boils down to gratitude, appreciating all that I have and acknowledging the divine grace that carries me through the challenges, be it Parkinson's or any other affliction. Even in the throes of battling this disease, I find joy in the richness of my life, blessed abundantly despite the adversities. My resolve is unwavering: I will depart this world with a heart overflowing with gratitude. Period.

THIRTY-SEVEN
FACING THE UNKNOWN AND I'M OK

"Who is among you who fears the LORD,
Who obeys the voice of His servant,
Who walks in darkness and has no light?
Let him trust in the name of the LORD and rely on his God.
Behold, all you who kindle a fire,
Who encircle yourselves with flaming arrows,
Walk in the light of your fire
And among the flaming arrows you have set ablaze.
This you will have from My hand:
You will lie down in torment."

— ISAIAH 50:10-11 NASB

Parkinson's still has me in its grip, bringing a whirlwind of uncertainties and what-ifs. Dwelling on these what-ifs tends to invite fear to sneak in through the back door of my mind. Instead of succumbing to fear, I've chosen to take steps that kick it to the curb. When I focus on the unknowns of the disease and its potential impact on me, my internal compass seems to go haywire, making it tempting to slip into victim mode rather than embracing victory.

To conquer fear, I've anchored my life on the rock-solid foundation of faith in Jesus Christ. One key pillar of this foundation is the overwhelming, incomprehensible love that Christ showers upon me. This love has granted me a genuine triumph over fear. Another essential part of this foundation is accepting that I don't need to have all the answers. I've deliberately chosen not to dwell on why Parkinson's found its way into my life or what might have been without its intrusion. Instead, I rest in the comforting truth that my God orchestrates all things for my benefit. Even Parkinson's isn't wasted in His grand plan when I surrender it to Him.

Navigating Parkinson's over the past five years, I've encountered a plethora of well-meaning suggestions and supposed cures, some even questioning my faith. There have been moments where I've been made to feel that if I had a smidgen more faith, I'd be miraculously healed. Despite having faith larger than a mustard seed, God has chosen a different path for my healing journey. Trusting that God can bring good out of Parkinson's not only in my life but also in the lives of others brings me profound peace. And the cherry on top? He walks with me through every step and every tremor, a constant companion on this unpredictable journey.

> "Trust in the LORD with all your heart
> And do not lean on your own understanding.
> In all your ways acknowledge Him,

PARKINSON'S & RECREATION 2

And He will make your paths straight.
Do not be wise in your own eyes;
Fear the LORD and turn away from evil.
It will be healing to your body
And refreshment to your bones."

— PROVERBS 3:5-8 NASB

In addition to those who question the depth of my faith, there are also those who advocate for putting all trust in science and human knowledge. It's almost like they're challenging me to have faith in *their* faith in the scientific method, which interestingly finds its origins in Christian faith. I firmly believe that God is the ultimate source of all goodness, including science itself. My wife and I are actively exploring the latest breakthrough treatments for neurological conditions, recognizing that all human wisdom ultimately stems from God.

I embrace life with all the symptoms of Parkinson's, cherishing precious moments with my family as the husband, father, and grandfather they have always known. What's the use of eradicating the disease's symptoms if it means losing who I truly am?

"The name of the LORD is a strong tower;
The righteous runs into it and is safe."

— PROVERBS 18:10 NASB

I'm unafraid of the mysteries ahead because I follow the one who holds all the answers in the universe, Jesus Christ. The Bible describes the name of the Lord as a fortress of safety where we can seek refuge. Each of God's names carries distinct characteristics that I turn to for solace depending on the challenges I face.

When I need comfort and protection, I embrace Him as the Shepherd.

In moments plagued by fear or self-doubt, I find strength in His name as Victory.

When my soul aches, I seek His healing touch as the Healer.

Feeling unworthy, I remember He Is My Righteousness and my identity as His beloved son.

Seeking forgiveness and peace of mind, I turn to His Holiness.

When my needs overwhelm me, I find solace in His Provision.

Amidst turmoil, His name as Peace brings serenity to my soul.

And in every situation, day or night, through the haze of Parkinson's, I find reassurance in His steadfast presence as I Am Here.

I may not know what tomorrow brings, but the comforting truth is that I don't have to face it alone. While Parkinson's may cast shadows, I choose not to rely on my own understanding but to trust in the light of Jesus Christ, the giver of life. Whether in life or death, I take solace in the fact that I am never abandoned. Even in my final moments, God will walk beside me. I trust that my journey ultimately leads me to His presence, a destination I confidently call home...and healing.

EPILOGUE

When I began writing this book, I had no idea where the journey would take me. No idea what level of suffering I might have to endure. No clear idea of what is reality and what is wishful thinking. But I have concluded that the quality of my life is trumped by the sanctity of my life.

What I mean is this: Every human life, regardless of race, status, talent, personality, or any other defining quality of humanity, is of intrinsic value. Whether I suffer the worst Parkinson's can do to me, or not, does not change the worth bestowed upon my life by Father God. My life was given to me by my God. It is to be fully lived in gratitude, regardless of my circumstances. I believe He will give me the grace to endure whatever Parkinson's brings my way, so I plan to live my life with joy during suffering while surrounded with the vast number of people who love me. Just as I value the human life that has just been conceived, I value the human life that is lived into old age. In fact, I place as much value on a life lived long, even with the pain that may bring, as I do the life of a newborn baby.

Parkinson's is certainly anything but a walk in the park. But that does not mean I have to settle for anything less than a joyful life. During the writing of this book, I asked my children and their spouses to feel free to let me know how Parkinson's had affected their lives. Honestly, I was taken aback by their bold honesty as they shared both their pain and their thoughts as to how I should adjust my attitude. A good slap in the face! A wake-up call. What I came away with was a healthier point of view than before, and I thought I had a very healthy point of view from the get-go!

As you have read the stories I have told, you have read the words of someone who is physically, emotionally, mentally, and spiritually suffering to some degree during the creation of this book. My hope is that you came away feeling what I feel as I wrote. Joy. Pure, unadulterated joy. I hope you laughed. I hope you cried. I hope you felt a sense of the fulfillment I feel even though Parkinson's is devastating.

I want you to be encouraged by a simple set of truths I live my life by. My God is bigger than Parkinson's. My God walks through Parkinson's with me. My God comforts me in my suffering and pain. My God fills my heart, my home, and my life with healing laughter. My God wastes absolutely nothing I experience. Not even my failures. That should speak volumes to us all.

Bottom line? I try to live my life from His point of view, and from there, I see nothing but hope and joy and the realization that I am never alone on this journey. My attitude is gratitude, even though my arm is tremoring so badly that my computer is about to fall off my lap. And that makes me laugh. Need I say more? Parkinson's is no walk in the park…or is it?

Be blessed and choose joy,
Dennis Jernigan

DID YOU ENJOY THIS BOOK?

Did you enjoy this book? You can make a big difference by leaving a review.

Reviews are one of the most important ways authors reach new readers. I don't have the funds to reach new people through advertising, but I have something more valuable: a group of individuals who support and believe in my ministry.

If you enjoyed this book, would you consider leaving an honest review? It doesn't need to be long. Your review will help other readers find this book.

To leave a review, simply visit your preferred book vendor where you purchased your copy of this book and leave your review.

BECOME A DJ INSIDER

Would you like to receive email newsletters from me? You'll receive periodic news, updates, offers, and prayer requests. There's no obligation and I'll never spam you. Don't miss out on another update! Visit www.dennisjernigan.com/newsletter to sign up.

You can also find me on Patreon to get daily devotions, music, new releases, and exclusive updates. Check out all the benefits at www.patreon.com/dennisjernigan

ALSO BY DENNIS JERNIGAN

FANTASY BOOKS BY DENNIS JERNIGAN
The Chronicles of Bren
A fantasy adventure series for young adults
Captured: The Chronicles of Bren: Book One
Sacrifice: The Chronicles of Bren: Book Two
Generations: The Chronicles of Bren: Book Three

The Bairns of Bren
Fantasy adventure series for young readers; for the young at heart!
Hide & Seek: The Bairns of Bren: Book One
The Light Eater: The Bairns of Bren: Book Two
The Puzzle: The Bairns of Bren: Book Three

SHORT STORIES FOR CHILDREN
The Incredible Growing Basketball Goal
Daddy's Song
The Christmas Dream

DENNIS JERNIGAN

OTHER BOOKS BY DENNIS JERNIGAN

Sing Over Me (autobiography)

Parkinson's' & Recreation - One Man's Journey Through Parkinson's…So Far

Renewing Your Mind: Identity and the Matter of Choice

The Middle of Nowhere

Daily Devotions For Kingdom Seekers, Vol I, II, and III

This Is My Destiny

Giant Killers: Crushing Strongholds, Securing Freedom in Your Life

The Short Life

MUSIC BY DENNIS JERNIGAN

Find all of Dennis Jernigan's 25+ music recordings at www.dennisjernigan.com or on most major streaming services.

Listen to The Dennis Jernigan podcast to hear the stories behind his songs.

WHO IS DENNIS JERNIGAN

Dennis Jernigan is a song writer and author who, with his wife Melinda, makes his home in northeastern Oklahoma very near where the stories were first inspired. They have raised nine children together and now enjoy many grandchildren. Foremost known for his Christian praise music, Jernigan has extended his creativity to the realm of authoring books.

Fantasy reached him with Hope during a very rough period in his life, and he feels a sense of urgency to write stories that will inspire others. The stories found within the pages of these books are his legacy to the generations to come.

For more information:
www.dennisjernigan.com
mail@dennisjernigan.com
(918)-781-1200
facebook.com/therealdennisjernigan
twitter.com/dennisjernigan
instagram.com/dennisjernigan
youtube.com/dennisjernigan

www.ingramcontent.com/pod-product-compliance
Lightning Source LLC
Chambersburg PA
CBHW070131080526
44586CB00015B/1646